Investing for Beginners: Why this is your last chance to buy cryptocurrency and experience 10X profits before it's too late

This book contains 5 manuscripts:

Cryptocurrency: Insider Secrets - 12 Exclusive Coins Under $1 with Potential for Huge Profits in 2018

Cryptocurrency: Insider Secrets 2 - 10 Exciting Crypto Projects Under $1 To Make You Wealthy in 2018

Ethereum: Beginners Bible - How You Can Profit from Trading & Investing in Ethereum - even if you're a complete novice

Cryptocurrency: Mining for Beginners - How You Can Make Up To $18,500 a Year Mining Coins From Home

Cryptocurrency: What you need to know about your taxes to save money and avoid a nasty surprise from the IRS

By Stephen Satoshi

Contents

Investing for Beginners: Why this is your last chance to buy cryptocurrency and experience 10X profits before it's too late

Cryptocurrency: Mining for Beginners

Cryptocurrency: Insider Secrets - 12 Exclusive Coins Under $1 with Potential for Huge Profits in 2018

By Stephen Satoshi

Financial Disclaimer:

I am not a financial advisor, this is not financial advice. This is not an investment guide nor investment advice. I am not recommending you buy any of the coins listed here. Any form of investment or trading is liable to lose you money. Do so at your own risk.

There is no single "best" investment to be made, in cryptocurrencies or otherwise. Anyone telling you so is deceiving you.

I am not affiliated with any coin or cryptocurrency mentioned in this book.

There is no "surefire coin" - one again, anyone telling you so is deceiving you.

With many coins, especially the smaller ones, the market is liable to the spread of misinformation.

Never invest more than you are willing to lose. Cryptocurrency is not a get rich quick scheme.

Affiliate Disclaimer:

Like cryptocurrency, I too believe in transparency and openness, and so I am disclosing that I've included certain products and links to those products on in this book that I will earn an affiliate commission for any purchases you make. Please note that I have not been given any free products, services or anything else by these companies in exchange for mentioning them in this book.

Accuracy Disclaimer:

All prices and market capitalizations are correct at the time of writing. Price and market cap information is sourced from coinmarketcap.com. All information in this eBook was derived from official sources where possible. Official sources meaning literature that is publicly available, provided by the development team for each cryptocurrency or company such as a company website or GitHub page. At the time of writing, some of the information is not available in English from official sources. In this case some of the information included in this eBook was obtained from unofficially translated whitepapers. Unofficially meaning either via computer translation, or human translation.

Introduction - The state of the cryptocurrency market in November 2017.

Wow, what a year it's been. Bitcoin reaching all time highs of $7,400. Ethereum skyrocketing nearly 3000% in just 9 months and even Litecoin finally broke through it's seemingly unbreakable 2013 barrier to hit almost $95. These are exciting times in the cryptocurrency sphere. And the best is yet to come.

There is a HUGE amount of hype in the cryptocurrency market right now. If you look at the Google trends data you'll see giant rises in the popularity of cryptocurrency related searches. If you look at r/cryptocurrency, the official cryptocurrency subreddit, the number of subscribers increased from 25,000 at the beginning of the year to over 134,000 at the time of writing.

Unfortunately, with this increase in popularity, there has been an uptick in poor information and it seems like everyday there's another heavily hyped ICO or cryptocurrency project. We've started to see ICOs advertising on social media, and using celebrity influence to try and tap into the mind of the general public. These are the types of investments I have deliberately LEFT OUT of this book. I don't want anyone investing based on hype alone, or a cool Facebook ad featuring Floyd Mayweather or The Game.

In the research phase of this book I looked at over 50 different small market cap cryptocurrencies, read the white papers, checked out the development teams and investigated where they had real world usage potential. From this initial group I narrowed down the final selection to 12 coins. These are my personal "best of the rest" in the cryptocurrency market, and the ones with most growth potential in 2018.

The price of these coins is not the singular reason you should invest in them. The market capitalization figure is arguably more important. For example, Ripple (XRP) tokens are priced around $0.18 but has a market cap of around $6 billion, making it a far more mature and structured asset, with less potential for large gains in the future.

In terms of general investing advice, diversification is important. However, if you have been in the cryptocurrency market for any length of time, you will know just how quickly things can move. This is even more so the case with these small market cap coins. My personal recommendation (just my recommendation - this is not financial advice) is that you have no more than **30%** of your total cryptocurrency portfolio in small cap coins like this. The rest should be placed in more stable investments such as Bitcoin and Ethereum.

One final note, this book is written with the assumption that you have some basic knowledge of cryptocurrency and the ideas surrounding it. If you're a complete cryptocurrency novice, I recommend one of my other books *Cryptocurrency: Beginners Bible* as it explains even the most elementary of cryptocurrency concepts.

Thanks,

Stephen

Factors to Consider Before Investing

While larger cryptocurrencies like Bitcoin, Ethereum and Litecoin have long track records and multiple real world functions, some of the coins mentioned in this book do not - hence their lower price.

There are a number of different variables to investigate before you undertake any investment, and cryptocurrency has its own set.

Proof of Concept (PoC)

In other words, does the technology have a working model, or is it still in a theoretical stage. Obviously more mature coins will have a higher value, with the more theoretical coins being a bigger risk. As the different coins here are in different stages of their life cycle, that is up for you to decide.

The Development Team

Who are the developers and what is their track record. Particularly within the cryptocurrency and blockchain space? Another thing to consider their record within the particular industry they are targeting.

The Utility Of The Coin

Ideas are great, but if the coin token itself doesn't have usage, then the true potential of the project must be questioned. This is especially true in the case of certain coins where the theory and market potential checks out, but the question of "why can I just use Bitcoin/Litecoin to do the same thing" is often raised.

The Roadmap

Roadmaps are important for short-term gains because they set out development targets for the coin. If these goals are reached and the products/platforms move from alpha to beta to a fully launched product, then that only means positive things for the coin and its value.

Which exchanges is the coin listed on

Many of these coins are still only available on smaller exchanges. Once the coin is listed on larger exchanges (for example Bittrex), the coin has greater visibility and this leads to a rise in value.

Mining Algorithm - Proof of Work vs. Proof of Stake

You'll notice later on when discussing individual coins that I talk about which mining algorithms are used. The two most popular are Proof of Work (PoW), used by Bitcoin and Proof of Stake (PoS), which will be used by Ethereum from Q4 2017 and beyond, and is currently used by a number of Ethereum based tokens.

In my previous book *Bitcoin: Beginners Bible* I discussed why I don't recommend mining as an effective method for obtaining cryptocurrency, for the regular user. That still holds true for the majority of the coins listed in this book, but it's important to understand why the difference in mining algorithm matters.

Why do we need mining?

We need mining to ensure a transaction (or block) is correctly validated, in order words, we need to ensure the same transaction doesn't occur twice - known as the double spending problem. As a reward for validating this transaction, miners are rewarded with a minute percentage of it (known as the network fee).

To put it bluntly, Proof of Work takes a lot more energy than Proof of Stake. A 2015 study showed that one Bitcoin transaction takes the equivalent daily energy of 1.57 US homes. Proof of Stake is also a fairer, more energy efficient system, which is a huge advantage for community based coins.

Minimizing Your Risk with Dollar Cost Averaging

One of the best ways to minimize your risk in a volatile market is to use what is known as 'dollar cost averaging'. This simply means dividing up your total planned investment and buying cryptocurrencies at regular intervals instead of all at once.

With dollar cost averaging, you are simply buying less of an asset (for this example, I will use Bitcoin) when the price is high, and more when the price is low. Your total exposure is less because you are only exposed to part of any decline in the market, as opposed to all of it with a lump sum investment. Your average cost per coin is therefore likely to be lower.

Let's use an example, both Jamal and Rachel have $1200 to invest in Bitcoin at the start of 2015. Jamal decides to invest all $1200 on January 1st, Rachel on the other hand is going to use dollar cost averaging. She will invest $100 on the 1st of each month, for a total of $1200. The prices used in this example are the actual Bitcoin trading prices as of those dates.

January 1st 2015 - $305.32

February 1st 2015 - $237.18

March 1st 2015 - $263.57

April 1st 2015 - $255.23

May 1st 2015 - $226.45

June 1st 2015 - $233.44

July 1st 2015 - $260.73

August 1st 2015 -$283.04

September 1st 2015 - $229.00

October 1st 2015 - $240.10

November 1st 2015 - $325.28

December 1st 2015 - $375.95

Jamal's total investment in LTC = 3.93 (1200/305.32)

Rachel's total investment in LTC = 4.55 (1200/269.60)

Price on January 1st 2016 - $433.57

Jamal's Portfolio Value = 3.93*433.57 = $1704.02

Rachel's Portfolio Value = 4.55*433.57 = $1974.37

Jamal's ROI = 42%

Rachel's ROI = 64.5%

So by using dollar cost averaging, Rachel's average BTC purchase price was $269.60, whereas Jamal bought a lump sum at $305.32. By having a lower average purchase price, Rachel's ROI is higher over time. Jamal bought his coins at the peak of the market before a prolonged downturn, whereas Rachel utilized this downturn to her advantage.

Remember, time in the market beats timing the market. Generally speaking, the longer you are invested in something, the better.

Why you shouldn't touch a coin in the initial Post-ICO period

I made a conscious decision not to include any cryptocurrencies that were within 1 month of the end of their ICO. This particular period is extremely volatile price wise, and not a good period for anyone to enter the market, especially if you are an inexperienced cryptocurrency investor.

The reason for this volatility is often linked to ICOs offering a pre-sale bonus for early investors, who then sell their bonus in the post-ICO period for a quick profit, which ends up causing the price to fall. Usually, once the month after the ICO has ended, the price tends to become more stable.

All of the coins discussed in this book have been out of the ICO period for at least 1 month (many for years). Investing during the ICO period is a different matter, if you choose to do so for future coins, I advise you to read any instructions carefully so you don't send any coins to the incorrect wallet address.

7 Giant Mistakes Guaranteed to Cost You Money

1. Not double checking all links (including the ones in this book)

Unfortunately, phishing scams are rife in the cryptocurrency space. Just this week, I saw 3 new ones either via email, paid search traffic (Google ads) or from reading about them on cryptocurrency message boards. Remember to check any link you click that is asking for you username, password or any other personal details.

2. Storing your cryptocurrency on an exchange

While rare, exchange attacks do happen, and cryptocurrency does get stolen. If you move your cryptocurrency off an exchange and into a private wallet, hackers cannot touch it (provided that wallet follows proper security measures). For each of the coins mentioned, I have included the appropriate wallet information for them.

3. Giving your private key to anyone

Your private key is what you need to send cryptocurrency from your wallet. You should never give this to anyone, for any reason. Keep it secure, preferably written on a piece of paper that is stored inside a physical safe. Never keep your private key on a server, and never enter it on a public Wi-Fi network.

4. Panic selling during a dip in the market

Unless you need the money to feed your family, there is ZERO reason to sell your cryptocurrency at a loss during a dip in the market. Remember, this investment should represent a small percentage of your overall investing portfolio, in other words - you can afford to take a small loss on paper. More often than not in the cryptocurrency market, waiting it out, and long term holding, is the best investment strategy.

5. Not using dollar cost averaging when buying

Time in the market beats timing the market. You can minimize your risk by using dollar cost averaging and spreading your investment out over time. This prevents getting burned by buying at the top of the market.

6. Not doing your research/due diligence

This book is designed to be a comprehensive introduction to these cryptocurrencies, but it is certainly not the only resource available. I encourage you to do your own research in addition to what I've provided in this book. The best source for information will come from the coin's own website and white paper (although at times white papers can read more like a press release than a technical document).

7. Borrowing money to invest in cryptocurrencies

This really should be obvious, but I've personally witnessed it too many times that I feel it needs to be reiterated. You should NEVER borrow money to invest in anything, let alone a market as volatile as cryptocurrency. Losing your own money is one thing, losing someone else's money is another. So, next time you're considering borrowing money from a bank, or using your student loan to invest - don't. Trust me, it's not worth it.

Bonus tip/mistake 7.5 - Checking the price of your investment on a daily basis

Just leave it alone - trust me

How to Buy Bitcoin

Gone are the days when buying Bitcoin was a time consuming and somewhat uncomfortable endeavor. Nowadays buying Bitcoin is a similar process to exchanging currency when you go on vacation.

There are two ways to buy Bitcoin, the first is to use fiat currency (USD, EUR, GBP etc.) to purchase cryptocurrency via an exchange. These exchanges function the same way as regular foreign currency exchanges do. The prices fluctuate on a daily basis, and like regular currency exchange markets - they are open 24/7. These exchanges make their money from charging a small fee for each transaction.

Some charge both buyers and sellers, some only charge a fee for buying. For security reasons, most of these exchanges will require you to verify your ID before allowing you to purchase cryptocurrency.

It is also important to note the type of payments each exchange supports. Some allow for debit/credit card payments whereas other only accept PayPal or bank wire transfers. Below are the three biggest and reputable currency exchanges for purchasing Bitcoin, Ethereum and other altcoins with fiat currency like US dollars, Euros or British Pounds.

Coinbase

Currently largest currency exchange in the world, Coinbase allows users to buy, sell and store cryptocurrency. Coinbase is undoubtedly the most beginner friendly exchange for anyone looking to get involved in the cryptocurrency market. They currently allow trading of Bitcoin, as well as, Ethereum and LiteCoin using fiat currency as a base. Known for their stellar security procedures and insurance policies regarding stored currency. The exchange also has a fully functioning iPhone and Android app for buying and selling on the go, very useful if you are looking to trade.

Once you are signed up and complete the identity verification procedures you can buy Bitcoin with your credit or debit card instantly.

Coinbase also recently launched the Coinbase Vault, which is a secure way of storing your cryptocurrency while still having it accessible to trade. The vault uses double email address + phone verification in order to access your funds. If you're planning on holding long-term, I still recommend offline storage - but as an intermediary option, the Vault is a step in the right direction.

If you sign up for Coinbase using this link, you will receive $10 worth of free Bitcoin after your first purchase of more than $100 worth of cryptocurrency.

http://bit.ly/10dollarbtc

Note, if you're going to be trading Bitcoin, I recommend doing so on Coinbase's partner platform GDax, which has lower fees.

Bittrex

Based and regulated in the USA, Bittrex is a great exchange to buy altcoins for Bitcoin or Ethereum. With over 190 different cryptocurrencies, it is the most comprehensive in terms of altcoin support.

Their support isn't as good as Coinbase's, and you'll have to transfer the coins to a wallet if you want to securely store them long-term, but for trading altcoins - you can't go wrong with Bittrex.

Poloniex

With more than 100 different cryptocurrencies available and data analysis for advanced traders, Poloniex is the most comprehensive exchange on the market. Low trading fees are another plus, this is a great place to trade your Bitcoin into other cryptocurrencies. If you have never purchased Bitcoin before, you will no be able to do so as Poloniex does not allow fiat currency deposits. Therefore, you will have to make your initial Bitcoin purchases on Coinbase or Kraken.

Buying Locally

The second way to buy Bitcoins in exchange for fiat currency is to locally purchase them in person. The advantage of this is that you may be able to get a marginally better price than by using an exchange. The other advantage is that users living in countries that don't have easy access to online exchanges can still buy coins in person. All transactions are protected by Escrow to prevent either party being scammed.

Website http://localbitcoins.com is the current market leader for local bitcoin transactions with sellers in over 15,000 cities around the world.

Transferring your newly purchased Bitcoin to your exchange of choice.

Once you have bought your Bitcoin from Coinbase/Kraken, you'll need to then transfer it over the Binance, Bittrex or whichever exchange your coin of choice is listed on. To do this, simply go to the exchange you need to transfer the coins to (e.g. Bittrex) and click on "deposit", choose BTC (remember to double check you've clicked the correct coin). This will generate an address that looks like this 1F1tAaz5x1HUXrCNLbtMDqcw6o5GNn4xqX

From there, go to your Coinbase/Kraken BTC wallet and select "send", then in the "recipient" section copy the BTC address of the new exchange. Double check the amount of BTC you are sending, then click send and the transfer will initiate. Most of the time transfers take around 10 minutes, however some exchanges take longer to process. Once your transfer is complete you can then exchange your BTC for any of the altcoins listed below.

Storing Your Coins - How to set up MyEtherWallet

Many of these coins are based on the Ethereum blockchain, and therefore use ERC20 tokens. Therefore, these tokens can be stored in Ethereum wallets. Wallets can be daunting to set up at first, so I recommend you use something simple to get started, the most convenient of these is MyEtherWallet.

Step-by-Step guide to setting up MyEtherWallet

1. Go to https://www.myetherwallet.com/

2. Enter a strong but easy to remember password. Do not forget it.

3. This encrypts (protects) your private key. It does not generate your private key. This password alone will not be enough to access your coins.

4. Click the "Generate Wallet" button.

5. Download your Keystore/UTC file & save this file to a USB drive.

6. This is the encrypted version of your private key. You need your password to access it. It is safer than your unencrypted private key but you must have your password to access it in the future.

7. Read the warning. If you understand it, click the "I understand. Continue" button.

8. Print your paper wallet backup and/or carefully hand-write the private key on a piece of paper.

9. If you are writing it, I recommend you write it 2 or 3 times. This decreases the chance your messy handwriting will prevent you from accessing your wallet later.

10. Copy & paste your address into a text document somewhere.

11. Search your address on https://etherscan.io/ Bookmark this page as this is how you can view your balance at any time

12. Send a small amount of any coin from your previous wallet or exchange to your new wallet - just to ensure you have everything correct

Hardware Wallets

Another safe, offline solution is to use a hardware wallet. The most popular of these being Trezor and Nano S. Both of these cost around $100, but represent a convenient, yet safe way to store your cryptocurrency. Further explanation of hardware wallets is in my first book *Cryptocurrency: Beginners Bible*.

12 Exclusive Coins Under $1 with Potential for Huge Profits

District0x (DNT)

Price at Time of Writing - $0.039

Market Cap at Time of Writing - $23,255,100

Available on:

BTC: Binance, Bittrex, Liqui

Where to store:

District0x is currently an ERC20 token and can be stored on My Ether Wallet. You can view how to add DNT as a custom token on https://etherscan.io/token/district0x

District0x has the goal of breaking the internet down into smaller, more manageable pieces. If you've ever seen the movie The Hunger Games, you'll remember each district was focused on a single task: District 7 was the lumber district, District 8 focused on textile production, District 9 with grain etc.

District0x plans to do the same thing with the blockchain technology and Decentralized Autonomous Organizations (DAO). Each district will have its own payment and invoicing system, along with complete self governance. The venture will use the Ethereum blockchain to run smart contracts.

What District0x has done to make to the process user friendly, is combine different necessary (like smart contracts and payment processing) elements into a package, so it's not essential for users to completely understand the technology behind the platform. At the core of every district is the ability to operate a market or a bulletin board application.

Currently, there are over 100 district ideas in play. Theoretically, it would allow an individual such as you or me to implement their own version of AirBNB, Craigslist or Uber, without having to go through a middleman like the current system has to. This in turn reduces transaction fees and makes the overall cost lower for all parties involved. There are no fees to create districts, which makes them available to everyone. Currently, refundable deposits are required to put forward a district proposal, once the district passes quality control checks (ensuring the district is not there for malicious intent), the deposit is refunded to the district creator.

One such idea already running is Ethlance, an online freelancing platform similar to Upwork or Fiverr, but without the large transaction fees. Interestingly enough, the District0x team has actually hired developers via Ethlance to help them execute the project.

Another promising proposal is ShipIt, which focuses on the multi-billion dollar shipping industry. The idea is to create a decentralized maritime logistics platform. The sheer number of transactions in this industry alone (trucking, forwarding, warehousing etc.) make this is a perfect foil for a blockchain solution.

The framework is in place, however the team needs to do more to gather traction and a userbase to utilize their own districts. The current team is small, with just 10 members, plus an additional advisor, but there will certainly be additions in the future as the project continues to grow. Progress reports are frequent and developments are regular posted on GitHub.

One interesting approach the District0x team are employing is creating a free "education portal" to inform the wider public about the platform, and the real world functionality of districts. They are doing this are they believe the current limiting factor is a general ignorance of the potential of the platform. The portal is scheduled for rollout in Q4 2017.

District0x tokens (DNT) can be used to fund project and stake voting rights in different districts, the more tokens one has, the greater of a say they have. The one issue here is a possible abuse of a "pay to play" system.

The decentralized element of District0x means there is no single point of failure, for example there is no single server that all of the individual districts run from. This ensures that targeted hacking attacks cannot take down the entire network.

Supply wise, there are 600 million DNT available, with a total projected supply of 1 billion. It should be noted that in the white paper, the District0x team does reserve the right to add additional coins to the total supply, however this is contingent on the exchange rate between ETH/USD. For example, if ETH's value declines significantly vs. USD, the team can add additional coins to account for this fluctuation. This isn't necessarily something to be concerned about (financial hedging occurs all the time in fiat markets), but it's definitely something worth nothing.

Listing on larger exchanges will help spike the price in the short term. The team are in ongoing discussions with large exchange Bittrex, and a listing on there could easily see price rises of 100%. Long term prices will be largely determined by the number of popular districts that are set up using the platform. The next two planned district launches are Name Bazaar and Meme Factory.

Neblio (NEBL)

Price at Time of Writing - $0.984

Market Cap at Time of Writing - $12,220,794

Available on:

BTC: Cryptopia

Where to store?

Wallets can be downloaded from https://nebl.io/wallets/

Based out of the USA, Neblio aims to provide a simple blockchain solution to the business sector. The project was born out of a need to simplify currently complex blockchain tools in order to achieve wider adoption within the business sector.

Taking into account blockchain solutions for transparent data, plus reliability and security owing to a lack of central server - the technology has a huge advantage for businesses over traditional methods. However, cost of maintenance, and difficulty of integration have made uptake in the business world somewhat slower than blockchain enthusiasts would like. Certain industries are waiting for more mature blockchain solutions to appear, rather than take a risk on technology that is unproven in their particularly sector. The Neblio team plan to streamline this process and make blockchain solutions more accessible for businesses as a whole.

A real world example of this would be a doctor's office needing to access patient records. Rather than use a traditional central database, that is liable to server downtime, or cyber attacks - they could use a blockchain solution which provides the same data, but without the risks. This same system could be used for any business that needs to utilize frequent audits, as the data would be unalterable with a record of who altered it and when.

Neblio plans to support current popular programming languages gives it a great advantage in this area. Developers in languages such as Python, Java, Javascript and PHP won't be forced to learn a new programming language to develop applications on the Neblio blockchain. This is an area that is vital if the platform wants to attract developers to Neblio versus other platforms. This also makes Neblio applications compatible with mobile devices running iOS or Android.

In terms of competitor coins, the space is extremely competitive. With giants such as Ethereum and Neo already occupying some of the real estate. Stratis is another big one, however, Stratis has had a year headstart and in terms of development, Neblio is already neck-and-neck.

The beta version of the Neblio network is currently scheduled for a launch in Q3 2018, with a larger scale marketing campaign due in Q2 of the same year. The team has been extremely active in developments, and recently both an iOS and Android wallet were both launched ahead of schedule.

Supply wise, there are approximately 12.5 million NEBL tokens in circulation currently, with a total supply of 13 million. NEBL tokens can be used as a means of exchange on the Neblio network

There is certainly a gap in the market for this type of blockchain solution. However, Neblio's future may lie with working within a specific industry, as the goal of solely providing broad "enterprise solution" is one that is susceptible to a large amount of competition, particularly from vast entities like Ethereum and Neo.

Bytom (BTM)

Price at Time of Writing - $0.069

Market Cap at Time of Writing - $80,324,168

Available on:

Fiat: Cryptopia (NZ)

BTC: Cryptopia, BTER (CN), Bit9 (CN)

Where to store?:

Bytom is currently an ERC20 token and can be stored on My Ether Wallet. You can view how to add Bytom as a custom token on Ethplorer via http://bit.ly/bytomwallet

Bytom is a true sleeper coin. Coming out of China, it's only natural that the coin has received initial comparisons to NEO (formerly Antshares), one of the most talked about cryptocurrencies of 2017.

Although their official Whitepaper is currently only available in Chinese, the roughly translated opening reads as "Bytom will not be another Bitcoin, or an Ethereum 2.0. Bytom is an intermediary connecting generalized blockchains with specialized blockchains." The whitepaper then goes on to discuss the idea of connecting physical and digital assets while resolving issues like compliance and trustworthiness.

In laymen's terms, Bytom has the potential for offline assets to be registered on the blockchain. In their own words, "bridging the online world and the atomic world". This bridging allows users to seamlessly swap between digital assets (like cryptocurrencies), and physical ones. This is something that no other cryptocurrency in development promises to utilize.

Real world applications for the technology include the management of income assets and dividend distribution for investors.

A very strong development team is headed up by Chiang Jia, who previously founded 8BTC - one of China's largest resources for cryptocurrency news and insights. Anyone who has been involved in the cryptocurrency market will understand just how important news from China is in affecting the price of Bitcoin and other crypto assets. The CEO was invited to speak at the 2017 Global Blockchain Summit.

Another determinant of the price is the viability of mining. Bytom has embraced the popular AI ASIC friendly mining algorithm. China is currently the world's largest base for cryptocurrency mining, with 70% of the entire mining work done in the Middle Kingdom. Part of Bytom's plan is to reward miners at a technological level as well as a financial one. CEO Jia stated in a June interview with 8BTC that "As for the mining industry, the outdated mining farm could be transformed into data center that provides AI hardware acceleration service." Chinese miners tend to support their own currencies, which is part of the reason for NEO's success in 2017. If Bytom can replicate this at even a fraction of the uptake, it will only mean good things going forward.

One particular thing to note about Bytom, is the team's dedication to continued, if somewhat slow progress. However, you can look at this in a positive light. Rather than succumbing to spending their entire budget on marketing like other coins, Bytom's roadmap is well laid out with realistic goals. You don't need to expect life changing developments within the next 6 months for example. But a solid alpha product in Q1 2018 could certainly lead to decent short term gains. Right now, the scheduled release of v1.0 of the Bytom blockchain is due in Q2 2018.

Other notable figures include Long Yu, a former Senior System Engineer at Alipay, a huge Chinese POS payment system (similar to Apple Pay or Samsung Pay).

In early September the Bytom team took home 2nd prize in a field of over 100 competitors in the 2017 Cosmos Hackathon, a blockchain network designed to solve problems like scalability and interoperability. 2nd Place is currently the best achievement from a Chinese team at the competition.

The roadmap shows that by early 2018, many of Bytom's most exciting features will be put to market, in beta form. A large press conference for the release of their alpha product is scheduled for Q1 2018.

Currently Bytom is in a unique place where there are no strict competitor coins.

The have been some blips in the development stages already, with Bytom removing the coin from Binance in mid August. However the coin is now listed on Cryptopia, which while being a small exchange compared to giants like Bittrex and Poloniex, does make it accessible to the US and western market. The Chinese market has easy access with direct BTN/CNY trades available on the BTC9 exchange. Those holding ETH can exchange it for Bytom at the BTER exchange.

Bytom's value comes from the fee each user will have to pay to use the Bytom blockchain. Holding Bytom coins essentially represents shares in the blockchain itself. Bytom believes strongly in this community based ownership model, and their concept of "distributed autonomy" is one that they hold dearly to the project. The aim is structure the management system for a balance between efficiency and fairness.

Circulating supply is high at 664 million BTN currently available, with a projected total supply of 2.1 billion BTN. Of this total supply, 7% is reserved for private equity groups and angel investors, whose funds will be used in the technology's initial development stages.

Overall, Bytom might not make any major price movements in the next 3 months, but as soon as 2018 rolls around, the coin has potential to make a big impact in the blockchain space.

Note: On some cryptocurrency exchanges, Bitmark will be listed as BTM, these two currencies as not related. Double check before executing a trade.

Golem (GNT)

Price at time of writing - $0.267

Market Cap at time of writing - $222,516,176

Available on:

Fiat: Yunbi (CN)

BTC: Poloniex, Bittrex, Liqui

Where to store?

Golem is an ERC20 token so can be stored in MyEtherWallet

Golen is a coin token, based on Ethereum blockchain technology. With nearly 10 months since the original ICO, Golem is somewhat of a granddad in the cryptocurrency world. Described by some commentators as the "AirBNB of computing", the value of the coin is centered around the tasks that can be accomplished using it.

The founders of the Golem Project refer to it as a "supercomputer", with the ability to interconnect with other computers for various purposes. These include scientific research, data analysis and cryptocurrency mining. For example, if your computer has unused, or idle power, using the Golem network, you can rent that power (hence the AirBNB comparison) to someone else who needs it. The user who needs the extra power, has the ability to access supercomputer levels of processing power for a fraction of the cost of actually owning the processing power themselves. Like other Ethereum based projects, the decentralized element provides an additional layer of security as there is no single point of failure on the network. The first use case of the network's alpha release was using shared processing power to produce a 3D CGI rendering.

One fantastic potential usage for this power is the ability for a company to prevent downtime during a urge of users. There are many examples of websites being down during periods of unusually high demand, such as waiting for a livestream of a popular event to start. One notable example of this is Rockstar's website crashing during the release of the Grand Theft Auto 4 trailer. Using idle power from other computers on the Golem network, has the potential to prevent issues like this from occurring in the future.

The growth of such services is currently in demand in the non-crypto space, with cloud computing services accounting for roughly $175 billion global turnover in 2015. For example, Amazon's Amazon Web Services (AWS) business is an increasing part of the online giant's overall holdings.

If you look at Golem vs. Traditional cryptocurrency mining, Golem is definitely a step ahead. Because it only utilizes idle power, there is no wasted energy, which traditional mining suffers from a lot of. Even for a casual user, the ability to offset some of their electricity costs is a big positive.

The ability for users to earn money for their unused computing power is, in theory, a no-brainer, however what remains to be seen is the practical application of the technology. The Golem team's lack of marketing visibility also appears to hurt the coins value in recent times. The lack of ability to buy GNT using fiat currency (such as USD) is also a drawback for the mass market, however for small cap coins, that is somewhat of a given at this stage of the overall cryptocurrency lifecycle.

Supply wise, 1 billion GNT tokens were generated during the ICO, and that is the sum total that will be available for the lifetime of the project. Tokens will be used as a transfer of value on the Golem network.

It should be noted that the technology is still very much in the early development stages and as of August 2017, the team are still looking for alpha testers for the project. The Golem Project has a very real possibility of petering out into nothing. On the flip side - there is tremendous potential for large future gains with the price of a coin still under $0.30.

Tron (TRX)

Price at time of writing - $0.0018

Market Cap at time of writing - $125,420,800

Available on:

BTC: Liqui

ETH: Liqui, EtherDelta

Even in small and medium cap cryptocurrencies, Tron is a true wildcard. Lead by Justin Sun, known in China as "The next Jack Ma", and part of Forbes Asia 30 Under 30 - the project is one with wide reaching implications for the in-app currency movement.

You can think of Tron as both a facilitator for in-game or in-app transactions (also known as microtransactions) and as a way of increasing the value of your own content.

The biggest trend in video games for the past 5 years has been the rise in in-game microtransactions, also known as the pay-to-win model. This frustrates gamers as any assets they have built up in game 1, are not transferrable to game 2. For example, take the popular mobile game Clash of Clans. The game features a huge amount of microtransactions, and players have spent hundreds of dollars building up their in-game assets. Currently there are only very limited ways for him to sell those assets in exchange for money. Plus, if a new game comes out and the gamer wants to try it out, they'd have to start from the bottom and work their way up again. Tron would allow said gamer to transfer his Clash of Clans assets over to the new game in exchange for a small transaction fee.

Content creators can also use Tron as a payment system for their content. Similar to how YouTube users use Patreon donations as a method of making additional income from their content.

The development team continues to grow, and the recent announcement of one of Alibaba's (the Amazon of China) chief engineers joining the project is another coup for the Tron team.

The future of Tron will depends of two things. The first is adoption, which games will support TRX as a middleman for cross-game transactions? Secondly would these games choose TRX over the coins currently available like BTC or LTC. Like many of the coins mentioned in the book, they idea in theory is a multi-billion dollar one, but does the token have enough utility to warrant it?

Supply wise, Tron is huge. With over 40 billion TRX coins currently in circulation, with a projected total of 100 billion. However, as the coin is designed to facilitate microtransactions (fractions of a cent), a large supply is needed.

In a show of good faith, in early October 2017, the Tron team air dropped 500 TRX coins into the wallet of everyone with an account on the exchange liqui.io. Air drops like this have useful community building and general awareness effects.

Aeon (AEON)

Price at time of writing - $0.84

Market Cap at time of writing - $12,359,745

Available on:

BTC: Bittrex

If you've read my first book *Cryptocurrency: Beginners Bible*, you'll remember I talked about Monero (the price has risen 3x since the release) being the only truly private cryptocurrency currently on the planet. Well, that's no longer the case. You can think of Aeon as Monero's little brother. In a market of overhyped, overbought ICOs and heavily marketed copycat projects, AEON brings lightweight innovation - the coin is a mobile-friendly, decentralized digital currency.

The team behind Aeon feature some of the core Monero developers - in the words of Aeon's founders "everybody's main internet device continues to be their cellphone, a device with a low-powered CPU and limited available storage. AEON is about enabling this era, enabling an age where all people everywhere have the freedom to privately send and receive money with whatever gadget they already own."

By focusing on smaller transactions like this, Aeon aims to take a firm hold on the daily consumer market, all while offering a completely private service. So why the need for privacy? Frankly, many of us are sick and tired of our data being stored on central servers, privy to anyone that wants to take a look. Aeon uses cryptography to completely encrypt the information of both the sender and receiver in a transaction. Therefore, the identifying information of each user is not available on the blockchain itself. This is compounded with what is known as "ring signatures", which means the funds are untraceable.

Aeon will often be compared to Monero, however the faster blockchain verifications (thanks to their lighter weight Proof of Work algorithm) allow transaction to process faster, making it more useful for day-to-day use. You could look at the relationship similar to Litecoin's relationship with Bitcoin.

The lightweight features of Aeon allow users to run a full node on their mobile, this speeds up transactions due to no longer needing a third party app running a public node. Another addition area where Aeon shines is by using a limited amount of storage space on a given device, this reduces the likelihood of any age-based attacks on your mobile or laptop.

One area that could be seen as a drawback for Aeon is the lack of a publicly released roadmap. This is due to an extremely small development team, of officially just 1 person at the time of writing. However, Aeon's open source code is publicly available, and everyone is welcome to contribute to the project, in a similar vein to Monero - which benefited greatly from a enthusiastic community. A community generated development fund currently stands at over $400,000 - which is far higher than other coins with much larger market caps. This fund will be used to attract elite developers to the project in the short and medium term.

Supply wise, Aeon has a relatively small number of coins released at around 14.5 million. For those into mining, Aeon currently offers some of the better rewards in the cryptocurrency mining space, plus in theory their lightweight nodes could allow for efficient mobile mining (albeit for significantly reduced rewards).

Where Aeon's future growth may lie is a release their mobile wallet in the short term and wider adoption of private cryptocurrencies in the long term. This is one coin that certainly has gamechanging potential.

RISE (RISE)

Price at Time of Writing - $0.401

Market Cap at Time of Writing - $45,404,571

Available on:

Fiat: Litebit.eu (EUR)

BTC: Bittrex, YoBit

Where to store?

You can download RISE wallets for desktop (Windows, Mac and Linux) from the Rise website

http://rise.vision

RISE is an ecosystem for developers, businesses, tech startups, investors and device users. The platform offers decentralized applications and the creation of smart contracts. The platform aims to increase adoption of RISE versus competitor platforms by providing Software Development Kits (SDKs), so that RISE applications can be run on Windows, Mac and Linux. The platform also supports popular programming languages like Javascript, Python and Ruby. There's also a RISE investment platform where RISE holders can pool resources together to invest in projects.

Where RISE really shines is their "blockchain incubator" service for startup Decentralized Apps (DApps). These developers can use the RISE platform to develop their companies/coins, and RISE holders will be entitled to 20% of these coins when the product successfully launches. While RISE isn't the first cryptocurrency to offer a form of passive income like this, a 20% reward is far higher than competing coins.

The two current projects built using the RISE platform are Interlet and Chipz. Interlet is an Ethereum based person-to-person vacation platform that aims to compete with AirBNB, by charging a much lower fee to operate. Anyone who has used AirBNB in the past will know about often ridiculous fees (up to 20% of the vacation price) that AirBNB takes as a middleman, and Interlet plans to use this is a basis for providing competition.

The second project is Chipz, an online casino platform due for launch in Q1 2018. Those who hold RISE will be given a % of Chipz tokens based on how much RISE they hold at the time of launch. Chipz plans to integrate with the Waves platform so that holders of the token can directly exchange their Chipz for fiat currency, which in theory will make the casino a lot more accessible. A successful launch of Chipz will certainly mean good things for the price of RISE in the short term.

Competition wise, RISE can be compared to Ark and Lisk in broad terms. However, RISE offers token holders a much bigger share of DApp coins launched on the platform at 20% when compared to Ark's 5%.

The roadmap is an area where RISE is lacking when compared to other coins mentioned in this book. Projects are in the pipeline, including the release of Interlet, as well as a mobile friendly version of RISE. However, a lack of dates for these releases is something that the RISE team needs to address to inspire investor confidence.

That being said, the RISE team is a strong one, with 10 developers, many of which have a long and successful history in the blockchain and cryptocurrency space. One area I particularly like is the weekly release of a RISE newsletter, these 4 page posts give updates on the RISE ecosystem, as well as announcing team members, and any new projects in development. Easily digestible new bites like this are useful if you don't come from a tech or development background, or are more interested in the business side of things.

The RISE community continues to grow rapidly, and often times community driven initiatives can help maintain and increase the coin's value over time.

Supply wise, RISE currently has 114 million tokens in circulation. The utility of these tokens has already been discussed, and there are strong use cases both as voting tools and as a currency to be traded. The trading volume is very high for a coin of RISE's size, and this bodes well for it as an investment tool as it is less susceptible to price manipulation than coins with lower trading volumes.

Funfair (FUN)

Price at Time of Writing - $0.026

Market Cap at Time of Writing - $100,375,472

Where to store?

FUN tokens are ERC 20 tokens, so you can add them to MyEtherWallet by using the following information:

Address: 0xbbb1bd2d741f05e144e6c4517676a15554fd4b8d

Token symbol: FUN

Decimal places: 8

Funfair is a decentralized gaming platform powered by Ethereum smart contracts, based out of London and Singapore. Powering the creation of "smart casino", the platform is attempting to capitalize on the potential $40 billion a year online gambling industry, an industry which has increased by 50% since 2010 and in projected to increase by another 50% by 2020.

The platform's main aims are to facilitate the building of online casinos with 3D games that can be built with current technology (namely HTML5) for both desktop and mobile platforms. In terms of gas costs (Ethereum transactions fees), these will be up to 10x cheaper than current online casino platforms.

As the games are executed with the use of Ethereum smart contracts, their fairness is not in question. The random number generated is transparent on the blockchain so anyone can see the results are truly randomized, and not artificially in favor of the house. This ensures that no one is being cheated by the casino operator.

Cryptocurrency gaming in itself is not a new phenomenon, in fact Bitcoin casinos have been running for years. However, the fluctuations in the currency itself, along with notoriously slow payouts and lack of regulation, has yet to see mainstream adoption.

The development team is built largely of members with previous experience in game creation. Founder and Angel Investor Jez San has a storied history in the gaming sector and helped play a part in the creation of multi-million dollar selling video games like Star Fox, while recently his experience lies in the online gaming space at leading online poker website PKR.com, before leaving the site to focus on Funfair. These connections could play a vital role in the adoption of Funfair within the gaming space, which is undoubtedly the number one challenge it faces going forward.

There are already complete 3D games built using the platform, which means the technology is now firmly beyond the theoretical stage, and into the execution stage. The Funfair launch suite itself already has 6 games under construction, which will be used as playable prototypes at industry events.

It is important to note that Funfair's value will not just come from the operation of 1 casino. Licensing the software itself will potentially create thousands of online casinos, which in turn will be in significantly more revenue than a centralized model. However, the challenge of getting that initial casino to decide to use the platform is a large one.

The main problem that has previously plagued this sector the transaction fees that occur with every new game or spin. This has led to other blockchain casinos suffering from slow playing times and costly fees to play. After all, nobody wants to have to wait 30 seconds between blackjack hands or between dice rolls for roulette. There's also a limit with the number of players that can play at one time. Current technology has a general rule of about 10 players per table, whereas with blockchain technology, the number, in theory, is unlimited.

The transactions costs are estimated to be at a ridiculous $1 per hand for blockchain based blackjack games and $0.75 per bet on dice games. With typical bet sizes, this represents around 10% per hand. Transactions costs have a further effect, because of the house edge of casino games. Even with higher bets minimizing the cost per hand, the house edge + transaction costs are simply too large for the player to even have a chance of profiting in the long term. Funfair's aim to reduce these will lead to a much higher uptake from players. One of Funfair's key goals is to reduce player transaction costs to a much more manageable 0.1% per hand.

Supply wise, over 3 billion FUN tokens were generated in the ICO - with no further token due to be generated during Funfair's life cycle . The sounds like a large number, however it is important to note that many of this are designed to be "burned" as transaction fees for the games themselves.The FUN token value itself will be utilized in a number of ways. Including for playing the games themselves, paying affiliates (which is a significant part of the online casino industry), and paying the game creators themselves.

Mothership (MSP)

Price at Time of Writing - $0.167

Market Cap at Time of Writing - $23,389,520

Where to store?

MSP token are ERC20 tokens so can be stored on MyEtherWallet

Mothership is one of the most intriguing cryptocurrencies on the market today. Built on the Ethereum platform, the coin's aim is to make cryptocurrency markets accessible for EU companies and Estonian e-Residents.

To truly understand Mothership, it's important to first understand Estonian e-residency, and how that process works.

E-residency takes place in the form of an Estonian government issued "digital ID card", which is combined with an authorized digital signature. The signature is legally binding and allows anyone in the world to register an EU company online. This gives unprecedented access to the European market. In a time where previously repressed parts of the world are looking for ways to attract new business and investment, Estonia is certainly at the forefront of this movement.

Where Mothership comes in, is that for blockchain businesses, it allows incorporation in Estonia, with 100% remote online access. A bank account will be provided, which is then linked with the built-in cryptocurrency exchange. Estonia also offers 0% corporation tax for companies inside the e-residency scheme. This is an extremely attractive proposition for blockchain companies that were previously forced to operate in countries with less friendly regulation, both in terms of the legality of cryptocurrency based firms, and general business tax laws.

The project entails three parts. A cryptocurrency exchange with 24/7 access to the markets, which combined with automatic identification (linked to your e-residency) makes the transactions from cryptocurrency to fiat currency near instant. Anyone who has signed up to a cryptocurrency exchange will know the pains of having to wait days (or even sometimes months) for identity verification.

The built-in cryptocurrency wallet is connected to your e-residency, which provides an automatic digital signature, which in turn protects your funds from fraudulent activity.

The e-residency program continues to grow, and Estonia estimates more than 10 million e-residents by 2025. Government support is one area that many crypto-based assets lack, whereas Mothership has been truly embraced by the Estonian government.

The project's timeline is publically available to view on Trello. The short-term goals include launching the beta version of the MSP token market whereas the actual exchange itself is planned for a launch between Q1 and Q2 2018. This is also the time period where the team plans to launch the e-residence wallet.

Supply wise, there will are currently 140 million MSP tokens, with an additional 60 million planned in the future.

The inherent risk to the Mothership project is that they are not specifically offering anything *new* to the market. There are already hundreds of cryptocurrency exchanges. However, the tie-in with the e-residency scheme, and the instantaneous swapping between cryptocurrency and fiat makes the project an attractive one in the short-to-medium term at the very least.

OKCash (OK)

Price at Time of Writing - $0.317

Market Cap at Time of Writing - $23,143,613

Where to store?

You can download the official OKCash wallet (available for both desktop and Android) from https://okcash.org/

Available on:

Fiat: Litebit.eu (EUR)

BTC: Bittrex, Cryptopia

Dubbing itself "the future of cash", OKCash plans to operate a worldwide payment system for microtransactions. With no cross-border payments and near instant confirmation times, the platform plans to target those in countries where bank account usage is not widespread. In other words, people have the ability to make payments to one another without needing a bank account.

The low-fee system allows OKCash to be useful for small donations or even online tipping. These tips can be made public and donations can be made over social networks for greater visibility. This could even be used in the case of emergencies to transfer funds fast to those affected.

While other cryptocurrencies promise similar things with regard to microtransactions and quick payments, where OKCash shines is the extremely low payment fee. There is no fee to receive a payment and the current fee to send OK coins is just 0.0001 OK, or $0.00003

One cool feature of the OKCash wallet is a built-in encrypted messaging system to protect users privacy.

OKCash has seen some strong initial adoption, with over 136,000 OKCash wallets being created already, and more than 19,000 addresses holding at least 1000 OK coins.

The proof-of-stake mining algorithm ensures minimal wasted energy when compared to a traditional proof-of-work algorithm (used by Bitcoin). The decentralized model also allows anyone to contribute to the OKCash network.

The team's marketing efforts have been unique and quite successful so far. A focus on video games has led to OKCash being a prize in both Minecraft and FIFA tournaments so far, with more projects like this to come in the near future.

The development team, and their lack of public visibility is an area that OK is lacking in. Although their site lists more than 40 team members, all of them currently go by pseudonyms, which is not helpful if the coin wants to achieve wider adoption.

Supply wise, there are roughly 72 million OK in existence currently. This number is deliberately larger than some other currencies in order to facilitate micro payments.

Note: OKCash is not to be confused with the Chinese Bitcoin exchange OKCoin.cn - double check any news regarding OKCash

Status (SNT)

Price at Time of Writing - $0.022

Market Cap at Time of Writing - $76,414,847

Available on:

Fiat: BTC9 (CN), b8wang (CN)

BTC: Bittrex, Liqui

Where to store?

Status users ERC20 tokens so can be stored using MyEtherWallet.

Status is an intriguing project that focuses on the mobile space. Based out of Switzerland, it's a free, open source mobile client targeting Android and iOS. The platform itself is built on Ethereum technology. Currently the platform supported 30 languages including Chinese, Korean and Russian. The main focus of the Status project in terms of high level goals is providing a fully private platform, with focus on a lack of censorship and economic transparency.

Co-Founder Jarrad Hope stated "One way to think about Status is that it'll eventually serve as a sort of onramp or gateway so that everyday people can benefit from decentralized applications built on Ethereum, whilst simultaneously helping DApp developers to reach new users."

Status users can search and discover decentralized apps (DApps). Similar to how one would do so on the Apple Store or the Google Play Store on their smartphone now. Examples of these apps include the freelancing platform Ethlance and Ujo, which is a decentralized music licensing and distribution platform. Status definitely have first mover advantage when it comes to a platform like this.

The other main usage here would be a decentralized peer to peer trading market. Similar to how localbitcoins.com currently operates. If Status can provide this for Ethereum based tokens, it could potentially be a game changer for the platform as a whole.

The aim of all this is to provide a digital hub where users only need one identity, as opposed to various usernames, passwords and apps that are common in the current system.

Status also featurs a built-in messenger with encrypted messaging and the ability to send Ethereum payments between parties, as well as smart contracts. The team chose to focus on messaging first and foremost, as they believed that this was the best and most efficient way to achieve mass market potential. Instant messaging software also has the highest install, and lowest uninstall rate of any mobile software.

The community element is a strong core belief of the platform. Status tokens (SNT) can also be used to ask questions to prominent community members, similar to how one would ask questions on the website Quora. Users can set a minimum number of SNT required to send them a message. This could lead to the rise in "celebrity users" with high levels of SNT required to contact them.

The team also offers rewards for those who can uncover bugs in their code. So far, the team has developed a fully functioning alpha product, with the help of over 6,000 testers.

In terms of competitors,you can think of Whatsapp as being the application with broad similarities to Status. The growth and true potential of Status will depend on the adoption of DApps as a whole, because it's unlikely that it's true calling will be purely as a mass-adopted chat app like Whatsapp or WeChat. If the team can facilitate a DApp store, then there is indeed a lot of room for growth in the coming years. In terms of cryptocurrency based competitors, kik is the one that is likely to be competition to Status in the short term.

One thing to factor with Status, is that first time movers often do not have a long-term advantage. The growth of Status will depend solely on their ability to stay ahead of the market, which is tough when competitors could come in and exploit Status' weaknesses as a platform.

Unlike other cryptocurrency projects, Status was self-funded for the first two years of its life. Supply wise, Status has a total supply of 6 billion, with 41% of this being funds contributed by the public during their July ICO. Interestingly enough, their ICO was designed so that large investments could not dominate the holdings. The Status team actually refunded more ETH than they took in during the ICO period.

The team are very active on their Slack channel (which currently has over 15,000 members), which is something that can't be said for some of the other coins mentioned in this book. Like any complex project, transparency is always a good thing, especially in times when there may not be much to report on the development front.

In terms of roadmap, Status is aiming for a public release towards the end of 2018, or beginning of 2019 - making this a good opportunity to get involved before then. A beta release in the middle of 2018 would give a clearly indication of the long term potential of Status, both as a platform, and as a messaging system.

Tierion (TNT)

Price at Time of Writing - $0.081

Market Cap at Time of Writing - $34,638,811

Available on:

BTC: Liqui, HitBTC (CN),

ETH: EtherDelta

Tierion aims to use blockchain technology as a data verification platform. Using their open source timestamping proof Chainpoint - Tierion has the ability to verify the integrity of a file, record, or process - without having to rely on a third party.

The practical applications for this are widespread. The ability to issue digital receipts for purchases, insurance claims or stock trades, which act as an immutable proof of purchase is a great asset in fighting fraudulent chargebacks and fraudulent transaction claims.

For auditors, the ability to timestamp data with a proof of record will drastically lower the chances for people to go back into a database an alter it. For example, a situation like Enron would not be allowed to happen with data stored on the blockchain. Going one step further, the auditing industry as a whole faces a huge threat from blockchain solution such as Tierion

Medical records, legal records are other areas where blockchain's verification process could have great benefits for society at large in the future.

Many of the above examples are ones that don't just apply to Tierion, but blockchain technology as a whole. That being said - why Tierion?

The answer is simple, speed. Tierion's API lets developers add up to 100 records per second, this is far quicker than previous blockchain solutions. An additional big advantage is their usage of current technology to make the process user friendly. It is much easier to create data stores using HTML forms which are both desktop and mobile compatible, than it is to learn an entire new programming language just for this purpose. This bridge between generations of technology, has great usage potential in the blockchain space for the near future.

Another cool thing about Tierion is its integration with widely used applications such as Salesforce, Gmail, Google Docs, and Mailchimp.

Unlike many of the blockchain based firms in this book, Tierion also has a full functioning product, which you can actually sign up to use for free today. The free version is limited to 15,000 data records per month, which should be more than enough for the average home user. Obviously, from a business standpoint, the money will be made with the Enterprise versions of the software.

The project already has links with some larger multinational companies. An invitation to join Dutch electrical giant Phillips' Blockchain Lab, a thinktank dedicated to see how blockchain technology can be used in healthcare. January 2017 bought an announcement of a working agreement with Microsoft to use blockchain technology to prove data existence and validity.

The big question with Tierion, is the utility of the TNT token itself. Will TNT be adopted as part of the Tierion ecosystem, or will users still prefer to carry that their transactions using a different cryptocurrency.

First Blood (1ST)

Price at Time of Writing - $0.517

Market Cap at Time of Writing - $44,310,766

Available on:

BTC: Bittrex, Liqui

Built on the Ethereum platform and based out of Boston with heavy ties to China, First Blood focuses on the ever growing esports space. First Blood aims to build a blockchain support esports platform that will allow gamers from around the world to compete against one another for prizes.

The use of smart contracts will ensure all results are fair and just, and that no cheating can occur. For those not in the know, the esports world has been plagued by cheating scandals ever since cash prizes were first introduced.

Their marketing efforts have been solid to say the least, and their "from the ground up" marketing strategy includes offering sponsorships to video game live streamers.

In terms of game themselves, First Blood's main focus for now is on the extremely popular Multiplayer Online Battle Arena game DOTA2 - with other game support planned for the future

An already established relationship with blockchain video game developer MOLD was compounded by a huge announcement on October 2nd 2017.

"We are proud to announce we will be working with the Chinese Government and Chinese esports companies to organize esports tournaments!"

More specifically, they're going to be used by the General Administration of Sport of China., the government agency responsible for sports in China. In a statement on their website the team announced

"First Blood will be a partner for hosting the Chinese University Esports League (CUEL). CUEL is a huge competition in China and each year hundreds of thousands of students participate. The partnership with First Blood was put into place as CUEL aimed to reduce their overheard."

The full version of the platform isn't out yet, but previous developer updates have mentioned banning cheaters from the beta platform, which shows that the technology is working at a basic level at least.

Future plans for the coin include support for additional popular games such as League of Legends and Counter Strike: Global Offensive - making this coin one to watch as we move into 2018

2Give (2GIVE)

Price at Time of Writing - $0.0053

Market Cap at Time of Writing - $2,786,042

Available on:

BTC: YoBit, Bittrex

Where to store?

The 2Give team currently has desktop wallets for Windows and Mac available on their website. A Linux wallet is coming soon.

2Give (or GiveCoin 2.0) is a comparatively tiny project when compared to some of the larger ones discussed here like Bytom and Status. With a market cap of just under $3 million dollars, it's safe to say that this one is a long shot indeed, but it's one with a good cause at heart, which is why it made the cut for this book.

From the official website "2GIVE makes it easy to support your favorite non-profit or pro-social cause and can be used for "repaying it forward" through social tipping!" The coin is supported by the Strength in Numbers Foundation, a non-profit digital trust. The idea is that user can donate to their charity of choice, without giving a significant portion of the funds to a payment process, while simultaneously revealing their online identity.

As previously mentioned, 2Give is the newer version of what was known as GiveCoin. The reason for the switch is that GiveCoin suffered from "pool hoppers", miners who switched between mining chains because it was financially advantageous to do so. This led to a system where the top 2% of GiveCoin miners took home most of the mining profits. 2Give's switch to a Proof of Stake model allows fairness to be restored among the mining community.

2Give attracts miners with a social conscience with their reward system, which offers a 5% to miners and stakeholders who help keep the platform operational. Miners then get an additional 1% as a transaction fee for processing payments on the 2Give network.

Many online rumours are flying around regarding 2Give's partnership with a number of large companies, including online streaming service Twitch and even UNICEF. It should be noted that with a market cap as small as this, these rumours can and do have a significant effect on the price.

2Give has received some early adoption, including a partnership with the Japanese Bitcoin ATM network coinoutlet. Coinoutlet ATM users can now buy 2Give at any of the ATM's around the country.

Future plans for the coin include mobile wallets for both iOS and Android, as well as a real world "air drop" in which gift cards will be left in various location to spread awareness of 2Give. The growth of 2Give will be determined largely by the adoption of the idea from non-profits around the world. If larger ones do get involved, then 2Give tokens will therefore have more utility and increase in price accordingly.

Conclusion

Well there we have it. 12 altcoins under $1 that have HUGE potential for gains in the next 12-18 months.

I hope this information has been beneficial to you and has given you a foundation to invest some of the more unknown cryptocurrencies. There has never been a more exciting time for cryptocurrencies than right now, so there's no better time to get involved.

I encourage you to do additional research before investing in any of these, particularly by checking out the white papers on the individual coin websites, which will give you a much more in-depth look at the technology behind them.

Remember to invest wisely (with your own money), don't check your investments on a daily basis, and don't panic sell if you see a dip in the market.

I wish you the best of luck in the cryptocurrency market, and I hope you make a lot of money.

Thanks,

Stephen

Cryptocurrency: Insider Secrets 2 - 10 Exciting Crypto Projects Under $1 To Make You Wealthy in 2018

By Stephen Satoshi

Introduction - The current state of the cryptocurrency market

Well, there's never a dull day in the crypto market and the start to 2018 has been no exception. We've seen record highs hit in December and January for a number of coins. Bitcoin reached $19,800, Ethereum topped $1,000 for the first time and Ripple soared to above $3. Since then the news has been more muted, and the market has been moving sideways and downwards for the past couple of months. Now before you think it's all doom and gloom, let's take a few minutes to examine why this movement isn't the worst thing in the world, and what we can expect from the crypto market in the rest of the years.

First of all, we must examine what has been causing the recent price slides. There are a number of reasons for this. The first blow came when it was revealed that a number of credit cards companies were banning users from making cryptocurrency purchases on their cards. This is a step forward as it is in line with other financial instruments. For example, no licensed stock trading website will allow credit card deposits, so crypto applying the same rules is a move in a right direction.

Secondly, we had the federal investigations into Tether, the cryptocurrency that is pegged to the US dollar. In late January, the US Commodity Futures Trading Commision (CTFC) began an investigation into Bitfinex and Tether. Tether claimed that all of its coins were backed by actual US dollars held in reserve, but failed to prove this was the case. Tether nevertheless denied accusations. Bitfinex was dragged into the battle because both companies share the same CEO. This caused the price of crypto to drop as some commentators believed Tethers were being printed to artificially inflate Bitcoin prices. If this is indeed the case, then we as investors should be willing to accept short term losses for a more stable long term market.

The third and final piece of bad news came out of Japan. The Japanese Financial Services Agency fined 7 different cryptocurrency exchanges for not following regulatory rules. The same agency then ordered two other agencies to suspend business altogether. This move came after Tokyo-based firm Coincheck had $530 million worth of cryptocurrency stolen. This news caused the market to drop by 5.3% in a single day. Once again, we should encourage a crackdown on poorly run exchanges if it means long term market stability.

Now, let's get on to the good news. After a senate hearing on cryptocurrency, CFTC chairman Chris Giancarlo made a number of bullish statements on cryptocurrency and blockchain technology. Giancarlo's most poignant line was "We owe it to this new generation to respect their enthusiasm for virtual currencies, with a thoughtful and balanced response, and not a dismissive one." A stance like this from the head of one of the most powerful financial regulatory committees in the US is only going to be a positive - both for consumer and institutional investors. Giancarlo then went onto discussing the benefits of blockchain technology and even discussed the term "HODL" in his speech. Financial regulators will support cryptocurrencies if it means people can make money with them through non-nefarious means. If they have to step in to prevent theft, hacking and use for criminal activity, then so be it.

Speaking on institutional adoption, March brought news of the Coinbase Index Fund. I discuss this later on in this book and what it could mean for crypto going forward, but needless to say, any kind of large scale institutional adoption is only going to be a good thing for cryptocurrency as a whole.

So without further ado, let's move forward and examine some of the best cryptocurrency projects in 2018, and see exactly how you can get involved.

Thanks,

Stephen

Factors to Consider Before Investing

While larger cryptocurrencies like Bitcoin, Ethereum and Litecoin have long track records and multiple real world functions, some of the coins mentioned in this book do not - hence their lower price.

There are a number of different variables to investigate before you undertake any investment, and cryptocurrency has its own set.

Proof of Concept (PoC)

In other words, does the technology have a working model, or is it still in a theoretical stage. Obviously more mature coins will have a higher value, with the more theoretical coins being a bigger risk. As the different coins here are in different stages of their life cycle, that is up for you to decide.

The development team

Who are the developers and what is their track record? Particularly within the cryptocurrency and blockchain space. Another thing to consider is their record within the particular industry they are targeting.

The whitepaper

A good whitepaper discusses the technical aspects of the coin, in a way that the average investor can understand. Many low quality crypto projects take shortcuts in their whitepaper and tend to fill it with hypey language rather than actual technological information. If a whitepaper doesn't discuss exactly how the project works, then that is a huge red flag.

The utility of the token

Ideas are great, but if the coin token itself doesn't have usage, then the true potential of the project must be questioned. This is especially true in the case of certain coins where the theory and market potential checks out, but the question of "why can we just use Bitcoin/Litecoin to do the same thing" is often raised.

The roadmap

Roadmaps are important for short-term gains because they set out development targets for the coin. If these goals are reached and the products/platforms move from alpha to beta to a fully launched product, then that only means positive things for the coin and its value. If a team consistently meets targets on or before a deadline, then we can look at that as a positive sign.

Which exchanges the coin is listed on

Many of these coins are still only available on smaller exchanges. Once the coin is listed on larger exchanges (for example Binance), the coin has greater visibility and this leads to a rise in value.

Mining Algorithms - Proof of Work vs. Proof of Stake vs. Others

You'll notice later on when discussing individual coins that I sometimes talk about which mining algorithms are used. The two most popular are Proof of Work (PoW), used by Bitcoin and Proof of Stake (PoS), used by coins like Neo, Stellar Lumens, Ark and a number of Ethereum based tokens. Ethereum plans to move to Proof of Stake in 2018.

In my previous book *Bitcoin: Beginners Bible* I discussed why I don't recommend mining as an effective method for obtaining cryptocurrency, for the regular user. That still holds true for the majority of the coins listed in this book, but it's important to understand why the difference in mining algorithm matters.

Why do we need mining?

We need mining to ensure a transaction (or block) is correctly validated, in other words, we need to ensure the same transaction doesn't occur twice - known as the double spending problem. As a reward for validating this transaction, miners are rewarded with a tiny percentage of it (known as the network fee).

To put it bluntly, Proof of Work takes a lot more energy than Proof of Stake. A 2015 study showed that one Bitcoin transaction takes the equivalent daily energy of 1.57 US homes. Proof of Stake is also a fairer, more energy efficient system, which is a huge advantage for community based coins.

Other systems include Delegated Proof of Stake (DPoS), which is a more community based initiative. DPoS is where stakeholders vote for delegates to make decisions for them, allowing both parties to profit from those decisions.

How to Buy Bitcoin, Ethereum & Litecoin in Under 15 Minutes

Gone are the days when buying Bitcoin was a time consuming and somewhat uncomfortable endeavor. Nowadays buying Bitcoin is a similar process to exchanging currency when you go on vacation.

There are two ways to buy Bitcoin, the first is to use fiat currency (USD, Euros, GBP etc.) to purchase cryptocurrency via an exchange. These exchanges function the same way as regular foreign currency exchanges do. The prices fluctuate on a daily basis, and like regular currency exchange markets - they are open 24/7. These exchanges make their money from charging a small fee for each transaction.

Some charge both buyers and sellers, some only charge a fee for buying. For security reasons, most of these exchanges will require you to verify your ID before allowing you to purchase cryptocurrency.

It is also important to note the type of payments each exchange supports. Some allow for debit/credit card payments whereas other only accept PayPal or bank wire transfers. Below are the three biggest and reputable currency exchanges for purchasing Bitcoin, Ethereum and other altcoins with fiat currency like US dollars, Euros or British Pounds.

Coinbase

Currently largest currency exchange in the world, Coinbase allows users to buy, sell and store cryptocurrency. Coinbase is undoubtedly the most beginner friendly exchange for anyone looking to get involved in the cryptocurrency market. They currently allow trading of Bitcoin, as well as, Ethereum and LiteCoin using fiat currency as a base. As of January 1st 2018, you can now buy Bitcoin Cash on Coinbase as well. Known for their stellar security procedures and insurance policies regarding stored currency. The exchange also has a fully functioning iPhone and Android app for buying and selling on the go, very useful if you are looking to trade.

Once you are signed up and complete the identity verification procedures you can buy Bitcoin with your credit or debit card instantly.

Coinbase also recently launched the Coinbase Vault, which is a secure way of storing your cryptocurrency while still having it accessible to trade. The vault uses double email address + phone verification in order to access your funds. If you're planning on holding long-term, I still recommend offline storage - but as an intermediary option, the Vault is a step in the right direction.

If you sign up for Coinbase using this link, you will receive $10 worth of free Bitcoin after your first purchase of more than $100 worth of cryptocurrency.

http://bit.ly/10dollarbtc

Note, if you're going to be trading Bitcoin, I recommend doing so on Coinbase's partner platform GDax, which has lower fees.

How to buy Altcoins

The vat majority of cryptocurrency projects cannot be bought directly for fiat currency. They require you to buy Bitcoin or Ethereum first and then exchanging that into these altcoins.

Binance

My personal favorite altcoin exchange, and the one with the most liquidity on a number of coins. Binance has over 100 cryptocurrencies available, and nearly all of them now have both BTC and ETH trade pairings.

Their support is top notch, and probably the best of any exchange. You'll have to transfer the coins to a wallet if you want to securely store them long-term, but for buying and trading altcoins - you can't go wrong with Binance.

Poloniex

With more than 100 different cryptocurrencies available and data analysis for advanced traders, Poloniex is the most comprehensive exchange on the market. Low trading fees are another plus, this is a great place to trade your Bitcoin into other cryptocurrencies. If you have never purchased Bitcoin before, you will no be able to do so as Poloniex does not allow fiat currency deposits. Therefore, you will have to make your initial Bitcoin purchases on Coinbase or Kraken.

Other sites I have personally used to purchase cryptocurrency include Liqui and Cryptopia. Please do your due diligence when selecting which exchange to buy and store coins on, and ensure you are always typing the correct web address to avoid phishing sites.

Transferring your newly purchased Bitcoin to your exchange of choice.

Once you have bought your Bitcoin from Coinbase/Kraken, you'll need to then transfer it over to Binance, Bittrex or whichever exchange your coin of choice is listed on. To do this, simply go to the exchange you need to transfer the coins to (e.g. Bittrex) and click on "deposit", choose BTC (remember to double check you've clicked the correct coin). This will generate an address that looks like this 1F1tAaz5x1HUXrCNLbtMDqcw6o5GNn4xqX

From there, go to your Coinbase/Kraken BTC wallet and select "send", then in the "recipient" section copy the BTC address of the new exchange. Double check the amount of BTC you are sending, then click send and the transfer will initiate. Most of the time transfers take around 10 minutes, however, some exchanges take longer to process. Once your transfer is complete you can then exchange your BTC for any of the altcoins listed below.

10 High Potential Coins Under $1

Ambrosus (AMB)

Price at Time of Writing - $0.55

Market Cap at Time of Writing - $80,288,043

Available on:

BTC: Binance, Kucoin, Livecoin

ETH: Binance, Kucoin, RightBTC

Where to store:

AMB tokens are ERC20 tokens so you can store them in MyEtherWallet or other Ethereum wallets.

Ambrosus is another supply chain cryptocurrency project. This time based out of Switzerland and focused on two main market sectors, namely food and medicine. One of the core technology partners for the Ambrosus project is Parity Technologies.

By using real time sensors, linked to a blockchain, the project promises to monitor the distribution and food and medicine across the entire supply chain network. This will allow for anti-tampering monitoring as well as the enforcement of smart contracts to ensure the product reaches its end destination and an automatic payment is released based on the fulfillment of certain conditions.

For example, if you have a certain food that requires specific temperature, humidity and PH conditions to be met during transportation, a tracking device with a sensor that monitors these would be implemented in the container used to transport the goods. If all conditions are met when it reaches its end destination, then payment would automatically be released. If any of the conditions fail, the recipient would be notified in real time, and thus action could be taken accordingly.

There is also the issue of data storage, a blockchain solution means the data is publicly viewable so there are no issues regarding fraud, data hacking or manipulation.

Ambrosus' main asset at this time is the team behind its development. I would go as far as saying this is the best crypto development for a low market cap coin that I've seen in a long time. Headed up by CEO Angel Versetti, who has a wide industry background including time spent working at the United Nations, where he was the youngest project leader in UN history, and the World Resources Forum. He also has a corporate background with both financial firm Bloomberg and technology giant Google. CTO Dr. Stefan Meyer has a vast supply chain and food industry background having previously led R&D projects at Swiss food giant Nestle. The rest of the team is made up of equal parts storied corporate history and successful blockchain developers. They are backed up with some world class advisors including Oliver Bussman, previously named CTO of The Year by the Wall Street Journal. As well as Prof. Malcolm J W Povey, one of Britain's leading experts in food sensor technology. In a world of fake bio pictures, and develop aliases, a team as open and transparent with a history like this is frankly unprecedented in any but the biggest cryptocurrency projects.

Like many cryptocurrency projects, the Ambrosus project is built using the Ethereum blockchain.

So how is the token valuable? One of the biggest reasons for the low price right now is that the token economics have not yet been finalized. The main usage for AMB will be to facilitate transactions in the Ambrosus network, like how ETH is used for Ethereum and Gas is used for Neo. There are talks of masternodes being available, so users could stake their AMB tokens to help run the network and receive dividends in return. There are current debates about whether there would be larger funds needed to run a node or smaller funds with a legal contract. The alternative for this would be a two tier system with masternodes running alongside peer nodes.

In terms of competitors, there are a number of companies and crypto projects in the supply chain space. Two of the bigger ones out of China are VeChain and WaltonChain. WaltonChain is an RFID centered project, so the two may not be directly comparable. RFID is a limited technology that is pretty much limited to one (albeit important) function. However, with sensor technology, Ambrosus has a much larger usage scope. For example, the ability to monitor temperature and humidity. The project could be compared to Modum in this respect.

Where Ambrosus may be able to win though is the Swiss factor. It is much easier for European companies to do business with a fellow European company than it is for them to deal with Chinese ones. There is also the legitimacy issue. Will a company needing specialized supply chain solutions opt for a partnership with a Swiss company, in a country that has a long standing history of quality and impartiality. Or a Chinese company with a previous history of manipulation, in the case of WaltonChain's fake social media giveaway scandal. Getting first mover advantage and partnerships with large companies is going to be huge in which one of these supply chain projects has the highest ceiling, but Ambrosus certainly has a geographical advantage over its competitors in this respect.

Overall, this is certainly a long-term project with potential industry leading ramifications. As such, I wouldn't expect any giant price movements in the coming months. But as we move forward into 2019, there could well be big things for the Ambrosus project.

Jibrel Network (JNT)

Price at Time of Writing - $0.47

Market Cap at Time of Writing - $71,386,200

Available on:

BTC: Bibox, HitBTC, Gate.io

ETH: Bibox, HitBTC, Gate.io

Where to store:

JNT tokens are ERC20 tokens and thus can be stored using MyEtherWallet or by using a Ledger Nano S.

An interesting project based out of Switzerland that aims to bridge the gap between cryptocurrency and traditional markets. Jibrel focuses on government backed cryptocurrencies, so cryptocurrencies issued by central banks, but that still are backed by blockchain technology. You can think of Jibrel as a "decentral bank" in this respect.

The reason for the project is that while blockchain technology is an incredibly useful innovation, it is still limited in real world implementation due to the lack of widespread adoption for cryptocurrency. Co-Founder Yazan Barghuti summed this up well by saying "People pay their bills, their loans, and their mortgages in dollars, Euros, and pounds. They don't pay them in ETH or BTC."

So by bridging the gap, and implementing smart contracts with non-cryptocurrency based currencies, it will allow optimized real world transactions. For example, if a smart contract had been implemented on sub-prime loans and ratings before the 2008 financial crisis, we could have seen adjustments made prior to the market crash based on the actual performance and makeup of these assets, rather than outside pressure which forced ratings agencies to keep these bonds at a AAA rating. This is just one of the wide ranging theoretical applications of the Jibrel Network project.

Barghuti argues that the end user doesn't necessarily need to know their money is backed by cryptocurrency. They would want to use it the same way they always have. Similar to how online banking doesn't change the currency you are using, it's just backed by a computer instead of a bank book.

How Jibrel plans to do this is by using what it calls CryptoDepository Receipts or CryDRs. This will allow traditional financial assets to be backed by the Jibrel Network's cryptography. So if you held $100 in silver, for example, a USD CryDR would back this up with $100 worth of JNT tokens. These CryDRs could also be used for trading.

As far as the user side of things goes, Jibrel aims to make things simple and this is where the jWallet and jCash make their mark. jWallet will function as a regular cryptocurrency wallet, but aims to bring greater security to the equation. You can also use the wallet to exchange cryptocurrency for fiat currency the same way you would do so on an exchange. This can help protect your assets if you are worried about cryptocurrency volatility.

Initially, the project will run using the Ethereum network. It is interesting to note that all jWallet's will run using Jibrel's own Ethereum nodes, so the end user doesn't have to connect themselves. While some may argue that this is a centralized model, one which cryptocurrency purists often fight against - there are practical implications for this. Barghuti argues that this approach is one that favors scalability more than anything else, stating "'Yeah, but the whole point about Bitcoin is it's off-grid, etc.' Okay you can stay off-grid, and that's a $500 billion market. But if you go on-grid, you can start tackling the issues with the $34 trillion global economy."

Initially, Jibrel will support 6 fiat currencies and 2 further money market instruments, with plans to roll out further currencies in the future. Ultimately it would seem that support for 20 or 30 currencies at the same time would be completely possible.

In terms of the team behind it. Co-Founders Yazan Burghati and Talal Tabbaa both have a strong financial services background, both having previously worked for the Big 4 firms. The technical chops come from Victor Mezrin, who previously ran one of the largest altcoin mining operations in the world.

Going forward, we have the release of the Jibrel institutional level banking platform scheduled for Q3 2018. This will be a big determinant of whether the project is successful or not. There are very few cryptocurrency projects this close to launching such a significant venture, and if it is successful in the early stages, I doubt that Jibrel will stay at its current price. The only competitor coin I can think of who are targeting financial institutions on this scale would be QASH, based out of Japan, who I covered in a previous book.

Then in Q4, the team has planned the full scale launch of the decentralized Jibrel Network. By this time we will have a solid grasp of whether the project is going to be a smash hit, or if it will fall by the wayside. Like any project that deals with banks, licensing is going to be a tricky hurdle to overcome. Different countries have different licensing procedures which take different lengths of time to pass - and we've seen how this can delay projects in the past in the case of debit card projects like Monaco.

Either way, Jibrel Network is an extremely exciting project which huge ramifications if it is successful. A breath of fresh air in the sense that it addresses the current limitations of blockchain technology and aims to give real world application without needing to reinvent the wheel. I wouldn't expect too much price movement in the next quarter, but by the end of the year, we will have a better idea of just how successful the project can be.

LoMoCoin (LMC)

Price at Time of Writing - $0.07

Market Cap at Time of Writing - $18,033,963

Available on:

BTC: Bittrex, CoinExchange

Where to store:

The native LoMo app has a built in cryptocurrency wallet

LoMoCoin, also known as LoMoStar is an intriguing project out of China that focuses on the incentivized shopping space.

First and foremost to truly understand the potential of the coin, you must understand the market it is targeting. Incentivized shopping, in other words, shopping via the use of digital coupons, is a huge deal in China and across Asia. Many businesses have social media accounts, for example on WeChat, China's biggest smartphone social media platform, in which they distribute coupons directly to customers. In other words, if you want to go to Dunkin Donuts, for example, you can follow their WeChat account and you will receive a coupon for doing so. As businesses compete for foot traffic, coupon based shopping is becoming more popular than ever.

The concept centers around the Chinese tradition of "red envelopes". Traditionally these are given out on special occasions like Chinese New Year and contain money. With LoMo, these envelopes would be in the form of discount codes for local stores.

For example, you are out shopping with friends, when suddenly you get a notification on your phone notifying you of a flash sale in a nearby store. This store might even be one of your favorites, and thus you've just scored a huge discount. From the store's perspective, performing airdrops like these builds brand loyalty, and gives them a chance to win new business that they would not previously have had access to.

LoMoStar is the app itself that the currency is distributed through. The app promises to be an all-in-one shopping and social platform where users can not only claim rewards and spend their cryptocurrency, but also perform their own airdrops with their friends. The app also has a built in cryptocurrency exchange, which while not revolutionary, will be convenience once increased adoption continues.

This kind of native advertising brings disruption to the traditional model of sponsored ads like Google AdWords and Facebook Ads. Year by year these are representing lower returns for those using them, as ad price increases and customers get more and more "overmarketed". In other words, they make a lot of money for Google and Facebook, but often represent poor ROI for the businesses running the ads.

The main driving force behind LoMo is the number of users downloading the app itself. As the user base becomes bigger, more businesses have incentives to do airdrops, and thus we can see somewhat of a snowball effect. Having a low barrier to entry "on-ramp" so to speak is a great way to attract those who are new to the cryptocurrency space. We have seen this in the past with coins like Ripple that became "accessible" due to their low price, despite their high market cap and limited room for growth going forward. Being able to take your first step into the crypto world just by downloading a smartphone app is a very simple solution for many users. Especially in target areas like Shanghai as well as other large Asian cities like Tokyo and Seoul.

Many users have reported earning over $100 USD worth of coins within the first few months of having the app on their phones. Which isn't bad seeing as you don't really have to do anything to get them. You can then transfer these tokens to more established cryptocurrencies like Bitcoin and Ethereum if you wish. Once again, this just reiterates the low barrier to entry effect and how this could be a huge bonus going forward.

The big question with this project is the same question we have with any project based in China. There is a certain risk involved with Chinese companies due to the cultural and regulatory differences when compared to the West. This is then compounded by the Chinese government's reactionary stance on cryptocurrency and often sweeping change in the law. For example, one of the biggest events in 2017 was when the government decided that Chinese citizens could not participate in ICOs, which led to a big downturn in the market. What further compounded this drop is that many media outlets in the West reported this event as "China bans cryptocurrency."

In terms of the team, I have to say I was very impressed. There are over 70 employees, many of whom have a solid blockchain background. CEO Xiong LiJian was previously involved in Litecoin mining development on both the hardware and software side.

Then we have to examine the potential for the project outside of China. Although the app currently has airdrops in multiple countries, it remains to be seen just how widespread adoption will be outside of the Middle Kingdom. That said, even if the idea is *only* successful within China, there will still be significant growth from the current price.

Overall, I like the idea of LoMo and their app. The social element could play a big part in bringing new users into the cryptocurrency space, which is vital if the technology is going to grow as we move forward. Low barriers to entry combined with incentivized rewards for using it, mean we could see industry changing ramifications. These are still early days, but if you are interested and want to see for yourself just how the project works, I recommend downloading the app on your iPhone or Android and check it out.

After all, if you aren't yet invested in crypto, this could be your first chance to own coins of your very own, without having to invest a single penny.

WePower (WPR)

Price at Time of Writing - $0.17

Market Cap at Time of Writing - $60,534,439

Available on:

BTC: Huobi, Liqui

ETH: Huobi, Liqui

Where to store:

WePower is an ERC20 token and can by stored in MyEtherWallet

An eco-friendly blockchain solution that focuses on the renewable energy sector. By creating a platform that allows green energy producers to interact with energy investors and green energy consumers, they have an incentive to keep creating renewable energy sources. For consumers, they would be able to purchase energy directly at a rate below the market price due to the lack of need for a middleman such as a government body. The project has already been listed as one of the Top 10 innovative energy initiatives in Europe by Fast Company magazine. The size of the renewable energy sector is growing every year with an estimated $200 billion of new investment annually. The team estimates the token market potential to be approximately $1.2 trillion per year.

By using blockchain technology and smart contract implementation, the project solves compliance issues such as a green energy owner selling energy that isn't theirs for example.

The tokens themselves will be tied to energy prices, and thus will naturally be more stable than other cryptocurrencies. This is important when we ask the question of "why can't the project just use BTC or ETH for transactions". By running the platform like this, it gives an inherent need for the WPR token and thus the WPR token itself has an intrinsic value, which is a big part of any cryptocurrency project.

The platform will use an auction model, in which producers put their tokens up for sale and buyers have 48 hours to bid on them. After these 48 hours have expired, non-token holders have the opportunity to buy them as well. This unique approach to trading green energy gives WePower a huge first mover advantage when it comes to the energy trading sector, particularly in the eco-friendly part of it.

The project's initial focus will be on the European market because EU member states all share a common energy agreement with regards to regulations. This agreement makes cross border energy trading relatively seamless. The project is currently in talks with the Lithuanian government about a joint venture with nationalized energy companies. Pilot projects are also underway in Estonia.

The renewable energy sector is one that continues to receive a lot of government support, for both blockchain and non-blockchain ventures. This support could be huge for WePower when we compare it to other cryptocurrencies projects that often run into red tape and bureaucracy. Having backing from a government, rather than having to fight it, will be vital if the project is to succeed.

In terms of the team behind the project, Co-Founder Nikolaj Martyniuk has over 10 years experience in the green energy sector. He is backed up by team members with FinTech backgrounds, energy consultants and blockchain experts.

Progress has been solid so far and a demo platform is already available on the WePower website for users to test out.

A big step for the project came in late February 2018 when it was announced that Binance included WePower in the latest round of voting for inclusion on the platform. This is a community poll where Binance members can vote on coins they want to see included on the platform. If the coin wins the poll then it will be included on Binance for trading. Early results indicate that the coin has been doing well in the polls and at the time of writing ranked number 2 behind Dentacoin.

Going forward, there are a number of near future dates on the roadmap that you need to be aware of. April 2018 will see a full scale testing of the project in Estonia, if this is successful then it will no doubt mean big things for the project. Especially in a space where many crypto projects are still firmly in the theoretical stage. Later testing is scheduled for Q4 2018 in Spain and Australia. The first actual distributed energy will be in December 2018. Then there are further expansion plans for 2019.

In conclusion, I like the approach of the project with the token system being particularly appealing. The idea of a green energy trading platform without middlemen is a fantastic application of blockchain technology. The need for the WPR token is another huge plus that just can't be overlooked. Listing on a larger exchange will be key in the short term, but the real challenge will be seeing if the testing phases in Estonia, Spain and Australia are successful. If they are, then this coin won't stay this low for long.

TheKey (TKY)

Price at Time of Writing - $0.0187

Market Cap at Time of Writing - Currently unknown due to lack of concrete information about circulating market supply. Based on estimated supply of 3.63 billion, we can make an approximate market cap estimation of around $65,000,000.

Available on:

BTC: Kucoin

ETH: Kucoin

NEO: Kucoin

Where to store:

TheKey uses the Neo protocol (NEP5) and thus you can store it in a Neo wallet. You can download one from the official Neo website https://neo.org/download - desktop, mobile and web wallets are available

Another project coming out of China, TheKey aims to use blockchain technology to create a decentralized national identification system.

This has many different uses in practical terms. One of the main ones being in healthcare. For example, individual citizens could apply for a smart identification card which would be linked to their cellphone. They could then use this to book doctor's appointments online. When they arrive at the hospital, the doctor could have automatic access to their medical records, and their insurance details. The ID could also be linked to a payment method, which could automatically pay for any medical bills required.

This then has anti-fraud ramifications, which could be useful for things like automatically ordering medication. For example, elderly patients could have medicine delivered to their home, so they wouldn't have to leave the house in order to get necessary medicines. Currently, there is no system in place which allows them to do this, because of concerns about people stealing identities to order medicine in order to resell it on the black market.

One of the first ICOs to use the Neo platform rather than Ethereum. ONCHAIN, the company behind Neo is also listed as a strategic partner for the project. The ICO itself was not without problems, as it went live at 2AM CET, which was immediately followed by a website crash and the donation amounts being filled without any chance for European investors to take part.

The coin boasts a number of big partnerships with Chinese companies, namely AliPay (AliBaba's payment platform). There are also plans to trial the technology in two pilot cities, with Jiaxing being the first one.

15 different patents have already been awarded by the Chinese State Intellectual Property Office (SIPO) which is promising to see and shows that the project clearly aims to have a larger scope than others.

The project is headed up by Catherine Li, who boasts an incredibly strong track record of entrepreneurship within China. In 2017 she was awarded Most Outstanding Women Entrepreneurs in China by the All-China Women's Federation. She previously worked at IMS Health, which provides big data solutions in the healthcare space. She is backed up by blockchain lead Ken Huang who worked at phone manufacturer Huawei as a Chief Blockchain Developer.

In terms of competition, the biggest project would be Civic. However, TheKey's focus on China is what makes it stand out. Chinese governments tend to favor internal projects rather than international ones. And if TheKey can garner some early adoption within China, this will make any nationwide or international rollout much easier. This is what sets it apart from the other identity verification blockchain projects. The other factor to remember, especially for a project like this, is that there doesn't only have to be "one winner", many competing projects can and will co-exist side by side, and take up a decent market share.

In terms of roadmap, the project mainnet is scheduled for release in December of 2018.

Right now the low price can be attributed to overall market conditions and lack of listing on a larger exchange. Kucoin is fairly solid and reliable but there just isn't the volume of a Binance or a Bittrex to support higher prices. A March announcement that the coin would be listed on Chinese exchange LBank, which is currently the 16th largest exchange in the world by volume, so this could have some additional growth effects in the short term.

The other drawback is the lack of literature available about the project in English. After studying the official website for some time, I still had a number of unanswered questions that I had to go to unofficial sources within the community to find the answers to. Once greater clarification is made in English on the official website, I have no doubt that more investors will be attracted to the project.

Out of all the projects I've discussed in this book, I'd say this is no doubt one of the more high-risk, high-reward type projects. The Chinese factor, and lack of English communication does mean we could all be mislead into believing the project is further along than it is. However, if you are willing to accept this, this could well be one of the biggest gainers of 2018 and beyond. From a blockchain enthusiast standpoint, it's interesting to see how scalable a NEP5 token will be when compared to one running on the Ethereum network. If TheKey fits your risk/reward profile then it is definitely a project worth checking out.

Note: The project is not to be confused with KeyCoin or SelfKey, which both use the (KEY) symbol. SelfKey in particular focuses on the same space so please ensure you are buying the correct token.

Oyster Pearl (PRL)

Price at Time of Writing - $0.97

Market Cap at Time of Writing - $72,546,189

Available on:

BTC: Kucoin, Cryptopia

ETH: Kucoin, CoinExchange, IDEX

NEO: Kucoin

Where to store:

PRL Tokens can be stored in MyEtherWallet. To create a custom token take the following steps.

Contract Address: 0x1844b21593262668B7248d0f57a220CaaBA46ab9

Symbol: PRL

Decimals: 18

Oyster Pearl addresses the issue of advertising on websites and provides a solution that satisfies both business owners and consumers who are browsing the websites. In their own words "Goodbye banner ads. Hello Oyster." The project combines decentralized storage and payment for content creators.

Currently, it is estimated that 50% of web users have some sort of ad blocking software installed on their computer or on their browser. Much of the other 50% have become somewhat immune to ads due to their frequency.

How it works is by using web visitors' excess computing power (CPU and GPU power) to store files on a decentralized ledger. This excess power provides Proof of Work which maintains the storage network. Site owners are then paid by the storage users, and in turn, web visitors get an ad-free browser experience.

The files themselves are stored on the IOTA tangle and uses Ethereum smart contracts in order to verify correct storage data. Because of all the data is encrypted and decentralized, fragments of files are stored rather than complete ones, this makes the files more secure than if they were stored on a centralized server like Dropbox for example. This model is open source, so the community can monitor it and ensure there is no nefarious action occurring at any time.

The project makes it extremely simple for businesses to adopt. In fact, all you need to do is add a single line of HTML code to your existing website. So any website that can run Javascript, can run the Oyster protocol. In theory, this should also provide little to no browser slow down or impacted computer performance on the user end either. This simplicity is quite remarkable in a space where many blockchain projects require developers to learn entirely new programming languages just to take advantage of a particular project.

There are a number of blockchain cloud storage projects, with a chief competitor being Storj, which is built entirely on the Ethereum blockchain. However, the main difference between the two is that Storj is strictly focused on storage, without the advertising incentives given to website owners. Siacoin is another competitor, although that project has run into numerous difficulties since their ICO last year. Oyster also has no plans to charge fees for downloading any stored files, whereas Sia does charge per download.

The team is headed up by anonymous developer Bruno Block. This person's anonymity is a cause for concern for some investors, while others are less worried about it. I should say that developers wishing to remain anonymous, while strange, is not uncommon in the crypto space. Much of the other team has come forward with their identities, and maintain public LinkedIn profiles. CTO Alex Firmani has a solid background in the cloud storage space, so industry experience is there. Many of the engineers on the project also have active GitHub profiles which is promising to see.

The main areas to monitor going forward are adoption. Will websites actually use the Oyster protocol versus the traditional advertising models like Google AdSense? Another area of caution would be whether the code added to the HTML will flag a site a malicious by certain anti-virus and anti-malware software.

A more technical concern would be the scalability of IOTA's Tangle network, which at this point has yet to be tested. The Oyster team have already said they will move to their own blockchain solution if the Tangle cannot live up to their needs. This is fine in theory, however, in practice, any switch will have a significant impact on the project.

In terms of roadmap, the team are currently in the Testnet A stage of thins, with Testnet B scheduled for later this year. Testnet B will be a public testnet. Mainnet is currently scheduled for April 2018 which is when Oyster will be fully up and running, and tweaks can be made if necessary.

Oyster Pearl tokens (PRL) are ERC20 tokens. After the latest coin burn there are around 98 million tokens in circulation. The token will be used to pay website owners who install the Oyster code on their site.

If you can overlook an anonymous figure heading the project up, Oyster Pearl is an ambitious project with great potential. Seeing a project running on IOTA's tangle is great to see from an adoption standpoint, and this is certainly a coin to look at closely.

ChainLink (LINK)

Price at Time of Writing - $0.51

Market Cap at Time of Writing - $179,183,250

Available on:

BTC: Binance, Huobi, OKEx

ETH: Binance, Huobi, OKEx

Where to store:

LINK tokens are ERC 20 tokens and can by stored on MyEtherWallet or other Ethereum wallets.

Based out of the US, ChainLink is one of the more ambitious projects out there and aims to create a platform where users can attach smart contracts to existing apps and data. This acts as a bridge between non-blockchain resources like bank accounts and data services and a public smart contract ledger. This would allow users to create contracts that perform the same function as real world binding agreements, but without the expensive middleman.

The entire theory behind the project is that current smart contract platform does not function with off-chain resources. Therefore a bridge is needed and that's where ChainLink comes into play. By acting as a bridge, the contract can be verified on the blockchain, without the data feeds needing to be on that blockchain as well.

In terms of use cases, there are many. For example, say you own a large warehouse that stores valuable goods. These goods are stolen one night, and you need to make an insurance claim. However, the insurance company is pushing back by claiming that the magnetic doors to the warehouse may not have been locked and thus this represents user error. By using ChainLink to connect the monitoring data for the doors, with your insurance contract - you would have an undisputed answer to the question. The same goes for an issue like a payment for a delayed flight, using ChainLink you have publicly verifiable data about how late the flight arrived and for what reason.

Maybe the biggest real world use case is in financial reporting. This could be anything from bond rates, interest rates and other derivatives. ChainLink would allow users to connect to external networks (like Bloomberg) in order to verify the correct data and thus the contract would pay out accordingly.

One of the bigger factors ChainLink has going for it is the ability to let users settle contracts in both fiat currency and LINK tokens. This will no doubt help real world adoption of the technology. The team even discusses this on their website and states that the current limitation of other smart contract platforms to mimic real-world financial agreements. As we saw int he case of the Jibrel Network, in the short to medium term, we will need some sort of bridging between traditional finance and cryptocurrency before we see widespread adoption of cryptocurrency only platforms.

The platform currently has partnerships in place with a number of other smart contract firms including zeppelin_os which powers over $1.5 billion worth of smart contracts. Another agreement is in place with Cornell University's Town Crier initiative - a patent pending system which verifies the security and trustworthiness of data.

An agreement is also in place with the payment network SWIFT. This came after the team won the Innotribe Industry Challenge in 2016. They are now working with SWIFT to develop a Proof of Concept - this will be centered around LINK smart contracts verified interest rates across data sources in order to generate a LIBOR average rate. The smart contract will then be used to generate secure payments based on this rate.

The main things holding back the project right now are the small development team. For the first 3 years of the project, there were only two developers, although CEO Sergey Nazarov confirmed at the end of 2017 that they had hired more members. Lack of updates from the team has been an issue, and a lack of public roadmap is also a cause for concern. For a project as mature as this one, greater public visibility is needed in the short term to reassure investors that everything is moving forward as they would have hoped.

In terms of the token itself. There are 1 billion LINK tokens in circulation, of which 350 million are in the current circulating supply. The team holds 30% with the other 70% split between Node Operators (needed to upkeep the network) and the general public. One interesting thing to note is that unlike other projects, there is no minimum staking requirement to become a node operator. Therefore this allows any users to participate in the network and earns passive income for doing so. Although the payout structure is yet to be finalized, this is certainly something to be aware of if you are interested in staking coins but don't have a huge amount of them.

Overall, ChainLink is a solid project that has proven real world application already.The partnerships in place are impressive, and the only thing holding it back is lack of transparency from the team. I would like to see them hire a full time press officer and marketing manager in order to better communicate the progress going forward. However, the technology alone makes this project well worth looking into.

SONM (SNM)

Price at Time of Writing - $0.15

Market Cap at Time of Writing - $54,959,826

Available on:

BTC: Binance, Tidex, Liqui

ETH: Binance, Liqui, Kucoin

Where to store:

SNM tokens are ERC 20 tokens and can by stored on MyEtherWallet or other Ethereum wallets.

SONM is a fascinating supercomputer project powered by the Ethereum blockchain, powered by miners using their idle computer resources. The project has already received some decent mainstream media attention and was voted #6 on the Top 10 Blockchain Projects To Watch Out For in 2018 by EntreprenEuros Magazine.

This has tremendous application including everything from web hosting to mobile and web applications, machine learning, scientific research, servers for hosting video games and video streaming.

This represents advantages to those needing to use these services when compared to the standard centralized solutions that we see today. Because the rental time on the supercomputer is completely flexible with no minimum amounts or minimum contract lengths - buyers only pay for the exact amount they need to use. If the task then takes fewer resources than the buyer anticipated, they will be refunded for the resources they did not need.

Miners have an incentive for powering the network as they will be paid in SNM tokens. You don't have to have a super powerful computer either, you can use your regular desktop or laptop. You can even use other devices with internet capabilities like your XBox and even your cellphone. Originally there were plans for SNM token holders to be rewarded with the network fees from the project, although this was dismissed due to potential regulatory issues (as the token would then be deemed a "security" by the SEC). There are still plans to reward token holders, but the economics have yet to be finalized. This isn't a major issue at this early stage, but it would be nice to see some additional information about this from the team within the next 6 months.

The project can be looked at as similar to Golem (GNT) which I discussed in the first edition of Cryptocurrency: Insider Secrets. Both aim to use idle computer resources to power supercomputers and thus we can view them as direct competitors. The one advantage SONM does have is that it plans to use the supercomputer for a wider variety of applications than just GPU rendering like the Golem project. In terms of development, SONM also has the advantage being further ahead on its roadmap. Once again, we should restate that there's no reason these two projects can co-exist with equal market shares.

Both projects share the same growing pains, namely, can the Ethereum network handle the sheer volume of transactions required to run a supercomputer like this. SONM's solution is to build their own sidechain (essentially an additional blockchain) which will process some of the transactions and lower the overall load on the Ethereum network. This sidechain will reduce all internal transaction costs to zero.

SONM has already announced a partnership with fellow Ethereum project Storj (discussed in Ethereum: Beginners Bible), the decentralized cloud storage platform. This will allow users to share files on the SONM platform. This additional step towards fully decentralized cloud computing is certainly an achievement going forward. Plus, it is always good to see blockchain project working together in order to gain mainstream adoption.

March brought news of another partnership, this time with blockchain AI platform DBrain. DBrain will be utilizing SONM's supercomputer to convert raw data into real world AI solutions for businesses around the world. SONM CEO Alexei Antonov stated, "Collaboration with Dbrain is an excellent way of demonstrating the possibilities of our project."

One thing SONM does extremely well is hitting their roadmap deadlines. From my research, I found they consistently hit project advancements on or before they were scheduled to. This demonstrates consistency from the team, and adds an extra layer of trustworthiness that other cryptocurrency projects simply do not have. Trust is vital in a space where the early years were dominated by news of theft, hackings and criminal activity.

As previously mentioned, users can buying resources using the SNM token, and those donating their idle computing power will be paid using the token as well. This already gives the token an intrinsic value, and use case - which is always one thing to look for when examining cryptocurrency projects.

In terms of roadmap, an MVP was released in late 2017 and a successful bug bounty round (rewarding users for finding bugs or errors in the code) occurred after that. A Windows client was also launched around this time. The first fee payouts are scheduled for Q2 2018. Followed by a full network release along with the full version of the SONM wallet on the Ethereum network - which is scheduled for July-August 2018.

In the short term, continued announcements of collaborations with other companies will be key to driving price action. In terms of growth potential, Golem currently has a market cap 6X higher than SONM's, and while the project is more mature, it seems that the SONM team are moving forward at a faster rate. This is one of the projects in the book that could have significant price action on both a short and long term basis.

OriginTrail (TRAC)

Price at Time of Writing - $0.18

Market Cap at Time of Writing - $48,535,364

Available on:

ETH: IDEx, HitBTC, ForkDelta

Where to store:

TRAC tokens are ERC 20 tokens and can by stored in MyEtherWallet and other Ethereum wallets.

OriginTrail is a blockchain project that focuses on the supply chain sector. The project was developed in order to combat the scalability problems that other decentralized supply chain projects are facing. The project has already won a number of plaudits in the industry including Walmart China's Food Safety Innovation and the Food + City People's Choice Award.

Supply chain data is often fragmented, as it comes from multiple different sources. This makes it difficult to track and monitor. OriginTrail aims to make this data more manageable without slowing down the process. You could potentially use this to track foos deliveries and authenticity of products when looking at their labels among other things. For example, a 2017 study showed to 70% of wine sold in China was fake. Meaning that it's origins were not what was stated on the bottle and was instead a mix of cheaper wine and water. This fake wine is then sold at a huge markup, which is often over 1000%. There have also been stories of rice contamination across the country. Another investigation, this time by the Wall Street Journal indicated that over one third of the fish sold in the United States was mislabeled. Needless to say, the current solutions are not offering the level of transparency that consumers require.

One very important thing to note is that the OriginTrail network can function across different blockchain protocols. This is known in the industry as being "blockchain agnostic". So it can be used in conjunction with projects built on Ethereum, Neo and IOTA for example, rather than just being limited to one of these at a time. This cross-operability is a huge step in any blockchain project, let alone one that has a lot of potential adoption like the supply chain sector. This would also allow large institutions (like Walmart for example) to build their own blockchain solutions and OriginTrail would be compatible with these. This could also potentially lead to partnerships with some of the biggest players in the industry.

This has many different applications across the sector including product authentication, supply chain management and food journey visibility. As well as backend functions like inventory management and production alert systems.

This is not a new initiative, and the core team has been performing supply chain tracing since 2013. However, they only began implementing blockchain technology in 2016.

The coin is backed up by a solid development team, each with a visible public profile on LinkedIn and extensive industry experience. Co-Founders Tomaz Levak and Ziga Drev both having backgrounds in supply chain management and tracing supply chains in Eurosope and the Middle East.

In terms of token use, TRAC tokens are a necessity for the network to function. The tokens are used to create nodes that hold up the network and process data transactions. Those who run nodes will be rewarded in the form of TRAC tokens. It is not yet confirmed if the project will use masternodes, and if so, how much these will be. Nor has any potential reward amount been confirmed yet. If you do have enough TRAC tokens to run a masternode, this would represent a fantastic passive income opportunity.

In terms of roadmap, the beta version of the testnet is currently scheduled for June. This will be the iron out any kinks and test OriginTrail's applications in various environments. After this, the mainnet is planned for Q3 2018 release.

Lack of a big exchange is the big thing holding back the price as of now. Not only are they not on the bigger exchanges like Binance or Bittrex, there aren't even any coin pairings on an exchange I would consider "mid-level" at this point.

OriginTrail is one of those cryptocurrency projects with industry changing ramifications IF they can achieve widespread adoption. It's a big if, as supply chain management is arguably the most competitive of the cryptocurrency project niches. However, their blockchain agnostic design may well be the "killer application" of this particular project. The ability to work with both open source and private blockchains is simply too be to be ignored, and thus this makes OriginTrail a project well worth looking into.

Note: BTC/TRAC trading is available on CoinFalcon (not to be confused with scam crypto lending platform Falcon Coin) - but the volume available is so low (<$1000 daily) I have not formally included it

Mercury Protocol (GMT)

Price at Time of Writing - $0.02

Market Cap at Time of Writing - $4,420,198

Available on:

ETH: ForkDelta

Where to store:

GMT tokens are ERC 20 tokens and can be stored in MyEtherWallet and other Ethereum wallets

By far the smallest crypto project discussed in this book, with a market cap of just under $4.5 million, Mercury Protocol is a decentralized communication platform. The project itself has been around for over 4 years, with blockchain implementation starting in 2016. On the website, Mercury Protocol lists famed billionaire Mark Cuban as an advisor. Cuban is an investor in Radical App LLC, the parent company behind the project.

The reasoning behind the project is that the current messaging model is centralized and relies on selling user data to advertisers for profit.

The platform offers demographic targeting as well, so advertisers can focus in on their audience, without wasting money by sending announcements to those who are not interested in what they are selling.

The main question you may be asking yourself at this point is - why would someone use Mercury Protocol built apps over other messaging apps that have their own internal economy such as WeChat? The answer to this is that GMT tokens are transferable across different Mercury Protocol apps. The theory behind this is that by allowing use across multiple platforms, it will create a network effect that will expand the user base and encourage widespread adoption. To give an example, imagine if there was a single token you could use on Facebook, Instagram, Whatsapp and Slack - this would be rather handy for both advertisers and users alike.

There are plans to make the entire platform open source in future released, so developers may then be able to make modifications and find any code bugs. There are concerns that this would lead to the rise of "clone platforms" - however, any clone platforms would need a large user base themselves to benefit from this.

GMT or Global Messaging Tokens can be used by network providers to make announcements on the network. The wider audience you want to make an announcement to, the more tokens it will cost. Users could be rewarded with tokens for watching adverts as well, which encourages them to use the platform in the first place. The team also believes that these tokens can incentivize good behavior on the platform and be used to eliminate trolling and online bullying. For example, users will be deducted tokens for harassment. The use of GMT versus BTC or ETH was done to minimize volatility from external factors. For example, if you buy a premium message with 1 ETH, then the price of ETH rises because of unrelated news, then you have just lost out. By using GMT, the price is generally only affected by activity within the Mercury Protocol network.

The token supply is fixed, so there is no mining involved. Users can earn more tokens by participating in the apps themselves.

In terms of roadmap, the mainnet release of the Dust app, the first built on the protocol, is scheduled for Q1 2018. You can download the beta version right now from the App Store or Google Play Store if you want to check it out for yourself. A second app known as Broadcast is currently in development.

The primary concern right now is the complete lack of any marketing effort from the core team. I understand they are working hard on the platform itself, but personally I believe that a coin should always be marketing itself, at least in order to stay relevant in a space that sees multiple projects pop up every day. Even a small weekly update on development progress would be a start. Once we move further into 2018, then talks of partnerships can be discussed and moved along.

In summary, this is no doubt a high risk project because of the small size and need for mass adoption to be successful. I think that it may see more success in niche markets rather than a full on social media 2.0 vision that some share. Even with niche market success though, there's no doubt the current token price and market cap would rise. They have a working product out which is a plus as well. All in all, for the low barrier to entry, it's a solid project with a lot of room to grow and should be looked at closely.

How to buy coins on Coinbase with zero transaction fees

Please note: This method only works for countries eligible for Revolut bank accounts which include the USA, Canada and the UK.

If you haven't heard of Revolut, it's a digital bank based in the UK. There have free currency transfers among 26 currencies - which is how we can use this to our benefit. You can even open an account in less than 30 seconds by using the Revolut app.

This is beneficial for Coinbase users because you can save up to 4% on each transaction by doing this, so if you're heavily involved in crypto you can potentially save hundreds of dollars per year.

Now, onto how Revolut can help you save money on cryptocurrency transactions.

Step 1: Send your native currency like GBP or USD, to your Revolut account via debit card. This step is easy and Revolut walks you through it when you set up an account. This transfer should be near instant.

Step 2: Exchange your native fiat currency to Euros on Revolut. Revolut has no transaction fees for this, so you get the market rate.

Step 3: Bank transfer your Euros from Revolut to Coinbase. This is the only step which is not instant, it takes 1 business day, so if you do it before 3PM EST you should get your coins before 9AM the next morning.

Step 4: Once your Euros are in your Coinbase account, transfer them to your GDAX wallet from Coinbase. If you're not familiar with GDax, it is Coinbase's sister platform designed for traders. Transfer between Coinbase and GDax are instant and free.

Step 5: Buy your coins on GDAX using Euro pairings, making sure to use Limit orders instead of Market orders, as these are free. If you use market orders, you will pay a 0.25% transaction fee.

Step 6: Transfer your newly purchased coins from GDAX to a personal wallet, or another exchange like Binance.

A Brand New Way to Buy Cryptocurrency Which Could Have Huge Market Ramifications

March brought news of an exciting development for those of you who want to get involved in cryptocurrency, but don't want to go through the process of buying and storing coins yourself.

I should note at the outset, this method is not viable for those of you only looking to buy a small amount of coins. This is strictly reserved for this with a lot of cash to spend.

US exchange Coinbase announced that they would be beginning the Coinbase Index Fund, aimed at becoming the "Dow of Cryptocurrencies". The fund will automatically diversify your cryptocurrency portfolio and rebalance it on a monthly basis. In the beginning, the fund will feature Bitcoin, Ethereum, Litecoin and Bitcoin Cash, any new coins added to Coinbase will automatically be added to the fund.

In the beginning stages, the fund will be offered to accredited US investors with assets of more than $1 million. Eventually, the threshold will be lowered in stages until the minimum investment is $10,000. There are also plans to roll the fund out across other geographical markets. The fund will charge a 3% management fee, which on the surface seems high. However, if you are looking for a truly passive crypto asset, this may well tick all your boxes.

How does this benefit the rest of the market? Any kind of institutional adoption is a positive sign. Last year we had 2 different Bitcoin ETFs rejected by the SEC on volatility grounds, so this is the next best option in the interim.

Things You Need to Be Aware of With Certain Cryptocurrency Channels on YouTube

For those of your planning to do extra research before buying coins, which is something I always recommend - YouTube is a great place to start. Many content creators do an in-depth analysis of coins in a similar fashion to what I do here. However, there are certain red flags you should look out for when determining how reliable the information on a certain channel is.

The creator has been paid to advertise coins in the past

Many of these channels, especially the ones with larger followings, are paid by the cryptocurrency teams to advertise the coin on their channel. There is no inherent problem with this, after all, it is just a form of advertising. The problem lies where the creator does not disclose they received payment to discuss the coin. And instead disguises this analysis in the form of a supposedly unbiased review.

The creator uses high pressure sales tactics or fake scarcity

Language such as "this coin will go up any day now" or "get in fast before you miss out", designed to spark a fear of missing out among the viewer, are rife in the crypto space. If a channel discusses a coin's price moreso than the project or team behind it, then you must be skeptical. If you find a channel that does this, then you have to take their "advice" with a pinch of salt.

The creator does not disclose their current holdings

There's nothing wrong with cryptocurrency personalities having their own portfolio, however, they should disclose whether they own a coin or not before discussing it in a public space.

The big one: They make promises of guaranteed returns

This one is the biggest red flag. There is a huge difference between discussing projects with potential and promising guaranteed returns if you invest in a certain project. This often is associated with coin lending platforms, such as BitConnect and Davor Coin, both of which exit scammed and caused anyone invested in them to lost 95% of their money. Remember this moreso than anything else. **There is no such thing as guaranteed returns in any investment - cryptocurrency or otherwise.**

Note: While writing this book, another lending platform Falcon Coin performed an exit scam, leaving investors with 98% losses on their initial investment.

Conclusion

And that's it - 10 more exciting altcoins under $1 that have fantastic potential for gains in the next 12 months and beyond.

I hope this information has been beneficial to you and has given you a foundation to invest some of the more unknown cryptocurrencies. Even with the rocky start to the year, there has never been a more exciting time for cryptocurrencies than right now. Even if you missed the boat with coins like Neo and Stellar, it's not too late.

As always, I encourage you to do additional research before investing in any of these, particularly by checking out the white papers on the individual coin websites, which will give you a much more in-depth look at the technology behind them.

Remember to invest wisely, and always with your own money. Never borrow money to invest in cryptocurrency or anything else. For your own sanity, don't check your investments on a daily basis. This is a volatile market, and you have to be willing to accept that if you are to make long term profits. Perhaps most importantly, don't panic sell if you see a dip in the market. From a personal standpoint, if I had sold during the crash caused by the famous Mt. Gox incident, in which Bitcoin lost over 60% of its value - I would be a much poorer man than I am today.

I wish you the best of luck in the cryptocurrency market, and I hope you make a lot of money.

Thanks,

Stephen

Ethereum: Beginners Bible - How You Can Profit from Trading & Investing in Ethereum - even if you're a complete novice

By Stephen Satoshi

Introduction

Wow, what a year it's been for Ethereum, and the cryptocurrency market as a whole. We've seen a 5000% price rise, passed 500,000 daily transactions, survived a Vitalik Buterin death rumor, and witnessed Ethereum truly arrive on the stage of the general public and cement itself as the number two cryptocurrency on the planet.

After opening the year sitting at a modest $7.98, with the market cap at a now unthinkably low $698 million, Ethereum continued to steadily rise and then saw its price explode by nearly 400% in just a 3 week period between May and June. After a few months of steady fluctuation between $250-$350, another breakout occured in mid-November and all time highs of over $500 were reached. At the time of writing, Ethereum's price sits at a cool $453, with a market cap of $45 billion. The Ethereum network now processes more than twice the amount of daily transactions as the Bitcoin network, despite Bitcoin's much higher notoriety.

It hasn't all been smooth sailing though, a June rumor, believed to have been started on the anonymous internet forum 4chan, claimed that Ethereum's founder Vitalik Buterin had been killed in a car crash. This led to an almost instant drop in market value of over $4 billion, which was recovered within a few short days.

So that begs the question, are we in a bubble? Only time will tell, but as I'll explain later on in this book, Ethereum is arguably the must bubbleproof cryptocurrency on the market itself for a variety of reasons. The main one being the sheer number of developments and potential use cases for the platform beyond just a means of exchanging value. The fundamental infrastructure of Ethereum has the potential to revolutionize the internet, plus how financial audits, and business transactions are conducted. That alone is enough for it to continue strong gains in the short and long term on the road to mass adoption. That's without discussing the other billion dollar industries it could potentially disrupt

It should also noted, that the cryptocurrency market as a whole is still only 20% as big as the tech market during the Dotcom crash ($300 billion vs. $1.75 trillion).

Thanks,

Stephen

Introduction to Ethereum - and what makes it so special

Ethereum was born in 2013 from a core team of 3 individuals: Vitalik Buterin, a Russian-Canadian programmer, Dr. Gavin Wood a British economist and game theory enthusiast, and Canadian entrepreneur Joseph Lubin. The fundamental idea behind Ethereum is that blockchain technology can be useful for things outside of just cryptocurrency. These included asset issuance, crowdfunding, domain registration, gambling, voting and prediction markets among innumerable other uses.

The main issue with blockchain platforms up to this point is that they were only designed to do one specific action, like Bitcoin for example, which only processes and verifies monetary transactions between two parties.

You can think of Ethereum as more like a smartphone. Smartphones are able to handle a variety of different types of application, with just one operating platform. Likewise for developers, if someone creates a smartphone application, then all they have to do is upload it to the app store, and users can download it without needing to buy additional hardware. Applications that run on Ethereum are known as Decentralized Apps (DApps).

What is a smart contract?

One of the fundamental ideas behind Ethereum is the use of self-executing smart contracts. We can think of a smart contract like a digital vending machine. A vending machine is a very basic way to ensure a financial agreement is upheld by two parties. Party a) the user and party b) the machine itself. Using a vending machine that dispenses Coke cans as an example. Let's say the cans cost $1.

- If we put it $1, and a coke comes out - successful transaction, and enforcement of the contract

- If we don't put in $1, and no coke comes out - successful enforcement of the contract

- If we don't put in $1, and a coke comes out - something has gone wrong, the contract hasn't been enforced correctly

In the case of a smart contract, the machine in question is a computer algorithm.

To use another example, you could set up a contract where the title deed of a home is transferred from a seller to a buyer, as soon as the buyer's money is sent to the seller. This transaction would usually require a third party to verify it (and thus incur an extra cost), but using smart contracts, the transaction executes automatically once both sides have upheld their part of the agreement, so a third party is not necessary. The lack of a third party, such as a bank or auditor, has the potential for huge cost savings across a wide variety of industries.

Is Ethereum the same as Bitcoin?

Not really. They are both distributed public blockchain networks, that much is true - but that's pretty much where the similarities end. As previously mentioned, Bitcoin only has a singular function which is a peer-to-peer electronic cash system to handle payments online between two parties. Bitcoin's blockchain is only used to track these payments and determine who owns how many coins.

Ethereum on the other hand is used as a platform for running many different kinds of decentralized applications. Unlike Bitcoin, Ethereum has multiple functions, beyond just functioning as an alternative method for payments. Ethereum tokens (known as Ether, although the terms are often used interchangeably) are used to process the running of the applications, essentially to "pay" for space on the Ethereum platform. A kind of fuel that is used to run the requested operations of the specific application and the execution of smart contracts.

To use an example of a smart contract versus just a transaction. We can compare Bitcoin to Ethereum.

Bitcoin can process a transaction of 1 Bitcoin (BTC) from Steve to Sarah. We can see how much Steve sent, and how much Sarah received.

What Ethereum can do is set up a contract where Steve will send Sarah 1BTC on a set date in the future, but only on the condition that Sarah has less than 10BTC in her Bitcoin wallet on that date. So if Sarah has more than 10BTC on that date, the contract knows it is should not execute, and transaction will not take place.

Another way you could look at Bitcoin vs. Ethereum is that Bitcoin is version 1.0 of a blockchain use case whereas Ethereum is version 2.0. Others like to use a Netscape vs. Google Chrome analogy.

So is Ethereum a programming language like Javascript or Ruby on Rails?

Again, not really. Ethereum is just a blockchain platform that applications can be built on. You can think of it more like an operating system like Windows or iOS. The apps and smart contracts themselves are programmed in a variety of languages such as Solidity.

How does Ethereum have value?

So if Ethereum isn't purely a cryptocurrency, how does it have value? The answer is that Ethereum tokens (ETH or ether) have value as long as the Ethereum network is up and running. The more programs that are running on the network, the more ETH are needed to keep the network running, and therefore the higher the value of ETH. You can think of this like the total amount of gas needed to run all the cars in the world. By buying Ethereum, you are showing faith in the network and the applications that are running on it.

Who is Vitalik Buterin?

While the identity of Bitcoin's "figurehead" Satoshi Nakamoto has never truly been revealed, and may not even be a single person - Ethereum followers can look firmly towards Vitalik Buterin as the leader for the project.

An unassuming looking 23 year old born in Russian, raised in Canada, with a love of unicorn t-shirts, mismatched socks and decentralization principles, Buterin's first entry to the cryptocurrency world was hearing about Bitcoin from his Father at the tender age of 17. He claims he dismissed the idea of cryptocurrency at first, believing there was no intrinsic value, but after quitting his World of Warcraft obsession, he sought something else to sink his time into.

Naturally, being a teenager and having somewhat of an "us versus them" mentality against large centralized institutions, he reexamined cryptocurrency and eventually began writing for a Bitcoin blog, in which he was paid 5BTC (then worth around $50) for each article. Buterin then went on to co-found Bitcoin Magazine, while studying at the University of Waterloo.

Buterin co-founded Ethereum at the tender age of 19 - with the aim of creating a network that could deliver multiple digital services without the need for a middle man by using smart contracts. This in turn would help regulate and govern the "double spending problem" that cryptocurrencies face.

In Buterin's own words, Ethereum was created to be a "general purpose blockchain", a move that some commentators called "impossibly ambitious", although many in the cryptocurrency space saw the move as revolutionary. A 2014 crowdsale raised 31,000 Bitcoins, which was trading at around $650 during the time, but crashed a few weeks later, leaving Buterin and his team with a much lower dollar value than they had previously anticipated. This didn't deter them and by spring of the following year, the early stages of the Ethereum project were online. Within just a few short years, his vision has already begun to take shape.

After co-founders Wood and Lubin left the project, Buterin continued as the sole figurehead of the Ethereum foundation.

On June 25th 2017, Buterin was the subject of a hoax regarding his death, believed to be started on 4chan. The rumor stated that Buterin had died in a fatal car crash and this caused $4 billion to be wiped from Ethereum's value as a number of parties panic sold their ETH. Within 12 hours, Buterin himself responded and proved that he was, in fact, alive.

Today, Buterin continues to be part-programmer, part-figurehead for the Ethereum project, albeit with a much larger team behind him. Dealing with the political and social consequences of running a giant blockchain project, as well as, working behind the scenes to improve the technology at the heart of it.

Challenges Ethereum faces going forward

Ethereum, like Bitcoin is now experiencing more and more of a network effect, and has cemented itself as the number 2 cryptocurrency going forward. It's addition onto popular newbie friendly exchange Coinbase has served as a positive for the mass market looking to get involved with cryptocurrencies. However, there a still a number of challenges Ethereum faces going forward on its path towards mass adoption.

Hacking Incidents

The 2016 DAO hacking incident

"The DAO" was a cryptocurrency that had an ICO in April of 2016, with the intention of providing the market with "smart locks" that essentially let people rent out their assets including cars and housing. Sort of a decentralized AirBNB model.

In the first 15 days of its ICO, The DAO raised over $100 million, and reached over $150 by the end of the funding period, which at the time was the largest amount raised by any ICO to date, and represented roughly 14% of all the ETH tokens on the open market. Although during the sale period, several commentators noted that the code was vulnerable to an attack.

On June 18th, a hacker moved 3.6 million ETH (then worth around $50 million) into a clone of the network. 2 days later, in a controversial move, the Ethereum community voted to hard fork the blockchain and restore the funds. This led to the creation of Ethereum Classic (traded as ETC), which maintains itself on the original blockchain.

The incident caused a 33% drop in Ethereum's value overnight. A year later, the thief's identity has still not been brought to light, although Ethereum itself has recovered.

The 2017 Parity wallet deletion incident

One of the stranger Ethereum events of 2017 was the freezing of roughly $200m dollars worth of Ethereum in the digital currency wallet Parity in November. A user managed to trigger an error during a wallet update which led to thousands of ETH being frozen. This error was caused by the user making himself the "owner" of one of Parity's smart contracts and deactivating the contract, which in turn froze the assets inside it.

Due to the way cryptocurrencies work, the only way these funds would be recoverable is to do a "hard fork" of the Ethereum blockchain when a certain fraction of miners refuse to update their ledgers, which would result in new ones being created. Hard forks themselves are risky, and usually have short term damaging affects on consumer confidence.

It should be noted that this was a problem with Parity's smart contracts, and not the Ethereum blockchain itself. There was a small dip in price (<3%) which showed that the market understood that this was a third party error. However, it does serve as a warning to keeping your crypto assets in a centrally controlled third party wallet.

As of the time of writing, total losses from the parity incident are unconfirmed, with most estimates ranging from $150 million to $300m dollars worth of ETH.

Motherboard news summed up the incident with a great analogy "*[The User] was jiggling door handles and when one door opened, they tried to close it and the whole house exploded.*"

With both of these hacking incidents it should be reiterated that the Ethereum network itself was not hacked. All networked systems are vulnerable to various kinds of attacks. The Ethereum network, which supports (depending on the price) around $1bn worth of ether, has not been hacked and is continuously executing many other smart contracts.

Vitalik as a Central Figurehead

Vitalik Buterin himself is another point where Ethereum could face issues going forward. Any central figurehead is going to be largely scrutinized and Buterin is no different. A comparison can be made to Litecoin, with founder Charlie Lee coming under continued pressure for comments he has made about various cryptocurrencies and the cryptocurrency space in general.

However, Buterin continues to take on the role of developer first and foremost rather than a traditional "frontman" so to speak. The argument could also be made that as the project is still very much in the early stages, a central figurehead is needed. It is likely that once Ethereum reaches more a "finalized" version, Buterin would be expected to move away from a public position.

Scalability

The problem with most larger cryptocurrencies is the problem of scalability. Can their networks handle a huge volume of transactions, without incurring high fees. For example, the average Bitcoin transaction now costs around $4 in network fees. Ethereum on the hand has lower amounts, but will need to keep these low, will still trying to handle a large volume of transactions. Vitalik Buterin outlined a plan at the BeyondBlock conference, for Ethereum to reach "Visa levels" of scalability, without compromising core values such as safety, security and decentralization. To give an example of how ambitious that is, Ethereum processes 15 transactions per second, compared to Visa's 45,000 per second.

Ethereum's solution to the scaling problem in the short term is the launch of the Raiden network. Raiden aims to shift the majority of transactions off of the main Ethereum blockchain by using a technique known as "sharding". This essentially breaks the transaction down into tiny pieces, allowing the pieces to run on different networks, and because the networks are all interlinked - the transaction can process the same way as it were on a single network.

While no specific time frame has been discussed for reaching this so-called "Visa level" - the launch of Raiden and continued updates to the Ethereum network could see much of Ethereum's scalability issues solved within the next 5 years.

Advice on investing in Ethereum and cryptocurrency

Beyond my usual advice of never invest more than you can afford to lose. There are a number of areas your should consider before you invest in Ethereum or any other cryptocurrency.

1.   Market Volatility

Cryptocurrency as a market is extremely volatile when compared to other financial markets such as derivatives and foreign exchange. Swings of 10% either way in a day are not uncommon, and smaller currencies can see their price double in a matter of hours (or in the case of Ethereum, rise 400% in just under 3 weeks). If you are a cautious investor, then cryptocurrency may not be for you, because with the potential for large gains comes an inherently larger risk. One additional note should be that the cryptocurrency market is open 24/7, and price moves can often happen while US or European citizens are asleep, thanks to the large volume of trading that occurs in China and South Korea. That said, Ethereum is one of the more stable cryptocurrencies.

2.   Dollar Cost Averaging

Before investing in cryptocurrency, it's wise to do some basic risk management. Traditional investing advice dictates that you should only invest 10% of your overall portfolio in high risk investments, and cryptocurrency definitely checks the box as a high risk investment.

Secondly, to remove your exposure to market volatitlity, you should employ what is known as dollar cost averaging when investing. That means, instead of investing a large lump sum at once, you divide that sum up and invest a little bit at equal time periods.

For example, instead of investing $12,000 all at once, break that $12,000 up and invest $1,000 every month over the course of the year.

The reason for this is that if the price suddenly dips 20% the day after your initial investment, your loss in terms of $ is lower if your use dollar cost averaging. You can then benefit from buying more at this new lower price the next month. So over the course of the year, your average purchase price is usually lower. I would strongly advise you utilize dollar cost averaging when you invest in cryptocurrency, or any financial market.

3. Diversification

If you do decide to invest in cryptocurrency, then Ethereum should by no means be your only holding. It should make up a large chunk of your portfolio, but diversifying is never a bad idea. Bitcoin of course is well worth looking into, as are the other smaller cap coins I discuss later on in this book. Once again, do you own research, and buy on fundamentals rather than hype.

4. Misinformation, fake news and FUD

Because the cryptocurrency market is still in its infancy, there are still very few reliable news sources, and unfortunately a larger number of unreliable ones. There's no bigger proof of this than looking back to the rumors of Vitalik Buterin's death in June 2017, which caused Ethereum's value to drop by $4 billion in just a few short hours.

The flipside of this is that mainstream major outlets do not employ cryptocurrency experts, and often will have traditional stock market analysts try to analyze the cryptocurrency market, which works in a completely different way. As such, there are often misleading headlines, poorly researched news stories, and downright incorrect technical information.

There are also those who intentionally spread misinformation about that cryptocurrency market, which causes Fear, Uncertainty & Doubt, known in the space as "FUD". FUD is different from pointing out legitimate flaws or challenges in cryptocurrency, as the sole intentional is to cause negative price movements, rather than spark actual discussion about the technology.

You should certainly stay informed with the latest Ethereum news, but there are better sources than others. Below are 4 websites that in my opinion offer the best, unbiased cryptocurrency news, without any of the hype or spin that you'll find on other websites.

http://coindesk.com

http://cointelegraph.com

https://coincenter.org - Focuses on cryptocurrency legislation

http://cryptopanic.org - A cryptocurrency news aggregator platform

I would also be wary of paid newsletters or websites that offer cryptocurrency investment advice. While many of these predictions and "tips" have grown in value in 2017, it should be noted that this is one of the biggest bull markets ever seen, so there are a disproportionately high number of winners this year alone. I advise you to do your own research first and foremost, before blindly putting your faith in one of these services.

5. Your reasons for investing

You should ask yourself if you believe in Ethereum, and blockchain technology as a whole, at a technological level before you invest. Blockchain is transforming the landscape of computing, finance and governance as we know it, but that doesn't necessarily mean all of these companies have functional or even useful products that the mass market will gladly adopt.

If you truly believe (as many do, including myself), that Ethereum and blockchain technology is here to stay, and that will correspond in higher prices, then by all means invest your money. However, if your motivations for investing are purely down to the fear of missing out, and the expectation of indefinite continuous price rises, then you may be better off keeping your money elsewhere.

6. **Don't day trade unless you know what you're doing, and have previous day trading experience**

While day trading may seem like the quickest way to make a lot of money, it's also the quickest way to lose a lot of money if you don't know what you're doing. If you've never day traded before, I would *not* recommend you start with something as volatile as cryptocurrency. Remember, the vast majority of day traders lose money.

Is Mining Ethereum worth it?

In one of my other books, *Bitcoin: Beginners Bible*, I outlined why I believed mining Bitcoins was a bad idea for the average person. I believe the same general advice is true for Ethereum, but for slightly different reasons.

While ASICs (powerful computer that are only built to perform one task, in this case cryptocurrency mining) are not available for Ethereum, which makes the network rewards higher for smaller miners, the electricity costs of mining in the Western world now offset these rewards. The Ethereum block reward was recently decreased from 5ETH per block to 3ETH per block. So once again, you will need a dedicated mining machine to make any sort of significant mining gains.

These dedicated machines require large capital investment, for example, the NVidia GTX1070, currently considered the best mining GPU available, costs $500, and for an efficient mining rig you'll need 6 of these. That's not even considering the other computer parts you'll require.

As a rough estimate for a US citizen mining at home, it would take 2 years for you to recoup your investment, and that is assuming mining rewards stay the same throughout those two years.

The opportunity cost of your investment is also money you could have just invested in Ethereum itself. For example, if you'd spent $5,000 on a mining rig at the start of the year, you'd have recouped roughly half of your initial investment by November. Whereas if you had invested that $5,000 in Ethereum tokens, your returns would be roughly $280,000.

There are other cryptocurrencies that are still profitable to mine at home, Monero being the main one as of November 2017, but as for Ethereum, you are better off putting your resources into direct investments.

How to buy Ethereum in less than 15 minutes

Okay, so you've done your reading and you're ready to jump into the world of cryptocurrency and buy some Ethereum of your very own. First of all, congratulations and welcome to the club. Now, let's get you some Ethereum.

Coinbase

Coinbase represents the most simple way to buy Ethereum for those living in the US, Canada, the UK and Australia, in exchange for your local fiat currency. Based out of the US and regulated by the SEC, Coinbase is undoubtedly the most trustworthy cryptocurrency exchange out there today. Rates are competitive with the other major cryptocurrency exchanges, and the verification requirements are solid without being a hassle.

Currently Coinbase supports both wire transfers and purchases by debit and credit card. Once you signup for a Coinbase account and verify your ID, you can buy Ethereum, along with Bitcoin and Litecoin, instantly with your debit or credit card.

You can also store your cryptocurrency in Coinbase's vault system. If you do this, you will have to pass 2 factor authentication in order to spend it. This is one step more secure than simply leaving it on the exchange, but still is not as secure as offline storage option such as MyEtherWallet.

Another advantage of Coinbase is that they have a fully functional mobile app that allows the buying and selling of cryptocurrency on the go.

Now, as a special bonus to you - if you sign up for Coinbase using this link, you will receive $10 worth of free Bitcoin after your first purchase of more than $100 worth of Bitcoin, Ethereum or Litecoin.

http://bit.ly/10dollarbtc

Once you have purchased your Ethereum, there are a number of other exchanges I recommend if you want to trade Ethereum, many smaller cap cryptocurrencies do not allow for direct exchanges with fiat currency like USD, so you'll have to buy Bitcoin or Ethereum from Coinbase first, then exchange that for the other cryptocurrencies.

Poloniex

With more than 100 different cryptocurrencies available and data analysis for advanced traders, Poloniex is arguably the most comprehensive exchange on the market. Low trading fees (between 0.1 and 0.25%) are another plus, which makes this is a great place to trade your Bitcoin or Ethereum into other cryptocurrencies. The big drawback of Poloniex is that it does not allow fiat currency deposits, so you will have to make your initial Bitcoin or Ethereum purchases on Coinbase.

EtherDelta

EtherDelta is especially useful for buying and selling ERC20 in exchange for Ethereum. While not the most aesthetically pleasing website to look at, EtherDelta employs Ethereum smart contracts to function as a decentralized Ethereum exchange. Currently there are over 100 different token available for purchase.

Exchanges I do not recommend

Kraken

I used to recommend Kraken as a solid Coinbase alternative, however their decreasing levels of customer support and increased downtime over the past 6 months has led me stop recommend them.

BitStamp

Questionable customer service decisions. One user reported a termination on an account with more than 60,000 EUR worth of ETH and XRP inside, but did not receive the funds back from Bitstamp, either in cryptocurrency or in fiat. While this issue, and others like it, are still ongoing, I cannot recommend the exchange.

Where to store your Ethereum - setting up your Ethereum

wallet

It is advisable that you do not keep any Ethereum (or any cryptocurrency for that matter), on a centralized exchange. The reason for this is that any cryptocurrency you store on an exchange is that directly controlled by you. This makes it vulnerable to attacks from third parties, and hacking incidents like the Mt. Gox hack of 2014.

.

Setting up Mist Wallet

Mist wallet is a simple way to store your Ethereum on your own personal computer rather than on a centralized exchange. This is more secure than an exchange, but for maximum security online storage (such as MyEtherWallet or a hardware wallet) is still recommended.

1. Go to https://github.com/ethereum/mist/releases and download the latest version for either PC, Mac or Linux

2. Install the wallet on your computer

3. Once installed click on "USE THE TEST NETWORK" and set your password. Use a unique password that you DO NOT use for any other website

4. Now you'll be able to see the wallets page and you balance should read 0.00ETH

5. Click on "Main account" - you will see your unique wallet address here, this will be 40 characters longer and will start start with 0x. If you share this address with someone, they will be able to send you Ether.

6. You can also send ETH from your account to any other ETH wallet address using Mist. You'll need your password to do so. When you do this you will see a confirmation number, you can check the transaction has processed correctly by copying this to http://testnet.etherscan.io/

How to set up an offline wallet with MyEtherWallet

All the coins in this book are based on the Ethereum blockchain, and therefore use ERC20 tokens. Therefore, these tokens can be stored in Ethereum wallets like regular ETH. Wallets can be daunting to set up at first, so I recommend you use something simple to get started, the most convenient of these is MyEtherWallet.

Step-by-Step guide to setting up MyEtherWallet

1. Go to https://www.myetherwallet.com/

2. Enter a strong but easy to remember password. Do not forget it.

3. This encrypts (protects) your private key. It does not generate your private key. This password alone will not be enough to access your coins.

4. Click the "Generate Wallet" button.

5. Download your Keystore/UTC file & save this file to a USB drive.

6. This is the encrypted version of your private key. You need your password to access it. It is safer than your unencrypted private key but you must have your password to access it in the future.

7. Read the warning. If you understand it, click the "I understand. Continue" button.

8. Print your paper wallet backup and/or carefully hand-write the private key on a piece of paper.

9. If you are writing it, I recommend you write it 2 or 3 times. This decreases the chance your messy handwriting will prevent you from accessing your wallet later.

10. Copy & paste your address into a text document somewhere.

11. Search your address on https://etherscan.io/ Bookmark this page as this is how you can view your balance at any time

12. Send a small amount of any coin from your previous wallet or exchange to your new wallet - just to ensure you have everything correct

Hardware Wallets

- Another safe, offline solution is to use a hardware wallet. The most popular of these being Trezor and Nano S. Both of these cost around $100, but represent a convenient, yet safe way to store your cryptocurrency.

To get your own Trezor wallet go to http://bit.ly/GetTrezorWallet

Cryptocurrencies built using Ethereum blockchain technology

It' not just Ethereum that relies on Ethereum technology. There are many other cryptocurrencies that use the same blockchain for specific use cases.

It may surprise you to know that there are currently **over 5000 ERC20 tokens.** One of the many positives of Ethereum technology is that it has made token creation extremely accessible, and as such the number of new tokens on the market has increased exponentially in the past 18 months.

Now obviously some are better than others, and in this section we'll examine a few of the more interesting ones and their potential use cases moving forward. Alongside each currency I've included its price and market cap at the time of writing, as well as, which cryptocurrency exchanges you can purchase it from and information about where to store it.

Augur (REP)

Price at Time of Writing - $20.19

Market Cap at Time of Writing - $219,749,200

Available on:

Fiat: Kraken

BTC: Poloniex, Bittrex, Liqui

Where to Store: Augur is an ERC20 token so can be stored in MyEtherWallet

Augur is a prediction market platform that uses Ethereum smart contracts to ensure correct payouts for correct predictions. Users can user it to predict real world events, and are rewarded if they are correct.

For example, you can predict the outcome of a Presidential election, a sporting event like the NBA finals or the winners of an Oscar award. Where Augur differs from a traditional gambling platform, is that instead of laying down a flat fee on an outcome at certain betting odds - you actually buy shares in an event.

For example, if you think Hillary Election would be elected President, and the market gives that a 50% chance, you essentially buy 50% of the shares of that outcome. If the market then moves, the odds become better than even, say 60%, your 50% share is now worth more than when you originally bought so you can sell it for a profit, before the event outcome is known.

Prediction markets like this have been proven to be more accurate over time than individuals. This phenomenon is known as "the wisdom of the crowd", or that a group of people is better on average at predicting events than any one person inside that group. This is especially true when those predicting are laying real money down on an event outcome.

Where Augur really shines though is that anyone can create their own prediction market. A small fee is required (to provide initial funding), and in return the creator of the market receives a percentage of all trading fees from that particular market. This decentralized approach is one that allows much lower fees than traditional, non-blockchain based prediction platforms.

This decentralization also adds an additional element of security, as the market cannot be subject of the manipulation of an individual, or small group of individuals like centralized markets. For example, someone has to actually report whether the event occured or not e.g. whether Clinton or Trump became President. With a centralized market, this can be subject to lies or outright corruption. With Augur, because each market has hundreds or even thousands of reporters, and the reports are publicly available for every to see, the correct result is always ensured. The Ethereum smart contracts also ensure regular, on-time payments for the correct amount - free from human error

Currently, a beta version of the platform is in development. This beta version will use virtual money only. This is done to test the coding of the smart contracts, and in case anything does go wrong in the beta stages, no one's funds are lost. The beta version of the AUGUR is also currently limited to markets with binary or "yes/no" outcomes, although there are plans to expand on this in the final version of the platform. The release date is currently scheduled for Q1 2018, although no formal release date has been announced yet.

Augur's tokens are known as reputation tokens or REP. 11 million were denominated during the ICO period, and this supply is designed to be fixed, so none can be mined. Those holding REP, and with a status set to "active" on the platform, will be expected to participate in the markets. If reporters do not report accurate results, they will be docked REP, which again ensures the legitimacy of the platform.

The team currently provides bi-weekly updates on their blog, part of these updates include offering REP in return for beta testers solving bugs in the code. Garnering community involvement like this has been hugely beneficial for other cryptocurrencies in the past.

Augur's price in the short term is likely to depend on how successful the launch of their beta platform is. Longer term, mass adoption versus traditional prediction markets is the main factor - will the masses see a blockchain solution as necessary in this particular use case?

TenX (PAY)

Price at Time of Writing - $2.26

Market Cap at Time of Writing - $209,278,662

Available on:

Fiat: Kraken

BTC: Bit-Z, Bittrex, Liqui

ETH: Bittrex, Liqui, EtherDelta

Where to store: Augur is an ERC20 token so can be stored in MyEtherWallet

Based out of Singapore, summarizing TenX can be best done with this quote from Inc. Magazine about the project

"TenX has figured out how to solve one of the biggest problems for people that are involved in cryptocurrency – actually spending the currency."

To elaborate, the TenX project is a platform that allows blockchain assets to be spent by individual users in the real world. One of the main issues with the growth of the cryptocurrency market as a whole, is with the constant additions of new token, how do uses actually spend them - without having to convert them back to Bitcoin or Ethereum, and then in some cases, back to fiat currency. The problem here lies with the transaction fees involved for these conversions, because they can add up fast, especially if you wish to carry out multiple transaction per day.

TenX plans to solve this by offering a debit card, that allows users to spend their cryptocurrencies at any regular point of sale system, this card is linked to a mobile wallet stored on their smartphone. Users can even spend their crypto assets directly via their smartphones at selected locations. Even today in the early stages of the project, the card is usable in over 200 countries, at over 36 million points of sale.

The key point to note here is that the cryptocurrencies stored in the TenX wallet are not converted to fiat currency until they are spent. This conversion then happens in real time. This also allows up to real-time currency conversions and the best possible foreign exchange rates and the lowest transaction fees.

The product has already completed a closed beta testing phase, with over 1,000 users testing the app in the real world, the total transaction volume during the beta phase was over $100,000. The beta tested version supported Bitcoin only, but the final platform aims to support Ethereum, along with ERC20 tokens and Dash in the short term, with support for additional cryptocurrencies planned in the long term. A public beta version is scheduled for release in Q4 2017, with a fully operational platform scheduled for Q2 2018.

Users in EU countries, along with select other European countries can now order TenX debit cards direct from the TenX website itself. There are plans to roll out the service in other countries, including the USA, in the coming months. With any payment platform like this, there are a number of compliance issues that have to be resolved - especially one that wishes to use the VISA debit card standard like TenX

There have been some issues however, with unprecedented demand for the cards themselves, which has in-turn caused a large backlog of orders. Currently the backlog stands at around 3 months, which is a major issue that will have to be resolved if the platform is going to have any sort of wider adoption.

TenX tokens (known as PAY) are used to incentivize usage of the platform. Users earn a 0.1% reward every time they use the app to spend their crypto assets, this reward is denominated in PAY. Currently this reward is distributed on a monthly basis, although there are plans to make this distribution as frequently as every hour in the future.

Holders of PAY tokens also receive a 0.5% reward based on the total transaction volume of the platform for the month. This reward is then multiplied by the number of PAY tokens each user has, so the more tokens one holds, the higher their reward.

During the ICO period, 51% of the total amount of PAY tokens were distributed to investors, with an additional 29% held back for further development of the platform. The team's long-term goal is to make 80% of the tokens available to the public, with the rest held by the founders and early developers.

One thing I particularly like about the TenX project is the team's commitment to wider cryptocurrency education through their YouTube channel. Cryptocurrency is still very much in the infant stages of its lifecycle, and any educational resources aimed at the general public can be looked at in a positive light.

The success of TenX going forward will depends on a number of factors. The first is competition, they aren't the only "cryptocurrency debit card" player in town. Monaco could be considered their main rival at this stage, although I'm sure that other similar projects will pop up in the near future. The second is the speed at which they can support various currencies in the app and card itself. Support for the big 3 cryptocurrencies (Bitcoin, Ethereum and Litecoin) would be huge for short term gains, and support for all ERC20 tokens would also be a positive as we move beyond 2018.

Storj (STORJ)

Price at Time of Writing - $0.678

Market Cap at Time of Writing - $70,896,782

Available on:

BTC: Binance, Bittrex, Poloniex

ETH: Binance, Bittrex, Liqui, Gate.io

Where to store: Storj is an ERC20 token so can be stored in MyEtherWallet

Storj (pronounced: storage) plans to take on the multi million dollar cloud storage industry with a decentralized blockchain solution. The team estimates that with a decentralized solution rather than a traditional model, cloud storage can be up to 10x faster and 50% less expensive.

Traditional cloud storage like say Dropbox, involves users uploading their files to a single, central server. Whereas with a decentralized model, these files are first encrypted to ensure their security, and then globally distributed across a set of storage nodes using blockchain technology.

The major problem that traditional centralized cloud storage companies face is that because there is one point of failure for the network, the network can suffer periodic downtime. Using a decentralized model, with the data effectively being stored in thousands of different locations, the network will not suffer from the downtime issues.

The other main issue that centralized storage faces is the security of the data itself. Once again, because there is a single point of entry to the server, there is also a single point of failure. This means no matter how good the encryption is, hackers could eventually get a hold of data. With a decentralized model, because the files are spread across thousands of different nodes

Another innovative function is the ability for users to effective rent out their unused hard drive space to users on the Storj network. This is known as Storj Share and users, known as "farmers" will be paid for their space in Storj tokens.

The Storj network is currently up and running, with a transparent pricing model, based only on what you use. Storage costs $0.015 per GB, per month with no minimum usage. So 100GB of storage would cost $1.50 per month. The platform has already attracted 25,000 users along with 19,000 farmers. An enterprise level model is also up and running, with an agreement already signed with a Fortune 500 company back in 2016.

One area that Storj may face trouble with is the hosting of illegal content via their service. The decentralized and encrypted nature of the platform makes it impossible to know exactly what kind of files are being hosted. The Storj team recognize this and are putting their faith in the userbase to use the service "within society's legal and ethical norms" and the ability for users to "graylist" certain content.

For example, those offering storage space could decide they do not want any pornographic material hosted using their space. You could argue that this is a centralized measure, but it should be noted that this only affects files hosted publicly, those hosted privately will be unaffected. Graylists will also be a strictly optional, opt-in required feature.

The coin has already received its fair share of support from big names in the Ethereum blockchain space, including Vitalik Buterin himself. This combined with a working product, make it an intriguing proposition as we move into 2018 and beyond.

Storj has also targeted an expansion into China to compete in their often difficult to penetrate cloud storage market. Regulations requiring overseas providers to partner with local companies caused Amazon to eventually sell $300m worth of its Chinese cloud storage assets to its local partner. Storj has partnered with Shanghai based startup Genaro in its own bid to expand into the large Chinese market.

Monaco (MCO)

Price at Time of Writing - $6.48

Market Cap at Time of Writing - $63,811,823

Available on:

BTC: Bittrex, Binance, Liqui

ETH: Bittrex, Binance, Liqui

Where to store: Monaco is an ERC20 token so can be stored in MyEtherWallet

Based out of Switzerland, Monaco aims to bridge fiat and cryptocurrency with an all-in-one debit card and mobile wallet app. The project should be looked at slightly differently to other cryptocurrency projects, as this one isn't strictly about cryptocurrency itself. You can look at Monaco more like a fintech project utilizing the cryptocurrency space.

Using their fair usage model, users won't be charged monthly or annual fees for holding the card. Monaco currently users VISA debit cards and the VISA payment platform so has access to over 40 million merchants worldwide. The project received official partnership with VISA in September 2017 and Monaco is now registered under the VISA Program Manager initiative which allows them further say in areas such as cashback rewards for their clients.

There are numerous features such as the card always using the local currency. So if you're someone who travels a lot, you'll have access to the official inter-bank exchange rate, rather than the consumer rate which is often 2-3% higher. Anyone who travels frequently will be able to understand that these savings add up quickly. Research has demonstrations this could represent savings of between $60-80 per $1000 spent.

The card also offers cryptocurrency cashback up to 2% with all purchases. Cashback cards are nothing new and have been around for decades, but Monaco represents the first one in the cryptocurrency space. The cashback will be in the form of Monaco (MCO) tokens. The cashback program is planned to offer higher rewards (of up to 10%) once wider adoption occurs.

The Monaco app can also be used to send instant payments to your friends and family, this can be done in multiple currencies including Bitcoin and Ethereum. On average, this will save 4% for international currency conversions when compared to regular banks.

Rollout of Monaco cards continues to rely on local compliance checks. The first cards will be shipped to those in Singapore after passing national governance tests in late October 2017. Over 17,000 cards have already been reserved and users can reserve their own by downloading the Monaco app for either Android or iOS. Demand is expected to be high and the Monaco team have already ordered over 500,000 physical cards.

Like most early stage projects, it hasn't been all smooth sailing for Monaco. A post-ICO price peak of $24 has been followed by steady declines throughout the year. This is partly due to initial ICO hype wearing off (pretty much every 2017 ICO has suffered from this), the other part is due to an issue with the smart contract mechanism in place. The original smart contract had to be re-worked in order to gain SEC compliance

Growth of Monaco is based firmly on passing compliance protocols across various markets. For example, their roadmap targets US approval within the first half of 2018, with European approval expected before then. Before then, news of Monaco being listed on more exchanges is what the community is looking for.

The team have experience in the payments space, for example the CFO is a former executive at MasterCard and they have advisers with previous experience at Visa and AWS.

The issue with Monaco going forward is that there is *a lot* of competition in the cryptocurrency debit card payments space already. I mentioned TenX earlier in this book, a project with similar intentions and there are other projects such as the UK based LBX along with TokenCard and Exscudo. There's no reason that a few of these cannot co-exist, but it will gradually be harder and harder to find a USP within the industry.

Selling points like better exchange rates and cashback are effectively a race to the bottom and there may have to be significant additions to the Monaco project for it to be the consensus leader in the space. We are still in the very early days of cryptocurrency though, and once the card itself rolls out - there are sure to be interesting developments both as a technology, and as a financial asset. Monaco is definitely one to watch as we enter 2018, with potential industry wide ramifications going into 2019 and beyond.

Aragon (ANT)

Price at Time of Writing - $1.67

Market Cap at Time of Writing - $57,369,782

Available on:

BTC: Bittrex, Liqui

ETH: Bittrex, Liqui

Where to Store: Aragon is an ERC20 token so can be stored in MyEtherWallet

Aragon aims to use Ethereum blockchain technology to remove the needs for unnecessary intermediaries in the business world. This concept of Decentralized Autonomous Organizations (DAOs) is a common one in the blockchain space. The number of third parties needed to create and maintain a company leads to market inefficiencies, lower profits, and hampers the ability of that company to provide the best possible product or service for its customers.

The aim of Aragon is to provide everything a person needs to run their organization. This includes services such as payroll, accounting and governance. This leads to greater company transparency, greater cost efficiency and the ability to safely alter a contract without the mound of excess paperwork that comes with traditional contracts.

The ease at which users can perform usually complex tasks like issuing company shares is a huge bonus for small organizations. The fact that all this is transparent as well acts as a built in fraud prevention system. This also applies to raising capital, using Aragon's stock sale voting, it has never been easier for companies to access the capital they require to run their business. Running all this on a publicly accessible blockchain makes budgeting, dividend sharing and general accounting practices incredibly simple.

The Aragon team is headed up by Luis Cuende, who has had a storied history in the blockchain space. Named Europe's best young programmer in 2011 and elected to the Forbes 30 Under 30 list - he previously worked on Blockchain startup Stampery

The test currently has an alpha product available, and 3,000 organizations have been built using the test network. A public beta version is currently scheduled for February 2018.

The main hurdles to overcome for Aragon going forward will be the adoption and trust from wider public, especially with regards to issues like contracts and arbitration. Any bugs in the network regarding this will need to be ironed out before a public release of the Aragon network. However, with 3,000 DAOs already on the testnet, this phase of the project continues to shine positive light on Aragon both as a vision, and as a legitimate platform going forward.

There are similar projects in the works, which isn't necessarily a bad thing as it shows that the general demand is there. Colony is another project that is more focused on the day to day operations of a company and could eventually be used as a module within the Aragon network as Aragon supports third party modules.

District0x (DNT)

Price at Time of Writing - $0.039

Market Cap at Time of Writing - $23,255,100

Available on:

BTC: Binance, Bittrex, Liqui

ETH: Binance, Liqui, Mercatox

Where to store:

District0x is currently an ERC20 token and can be stored on My Ether Wallet. You can view how to add DNT as a custom token on https://etherscan.io/token/district0x

District0x has the goal of breaking the internet down into smaller, more manageable pieces. If you've ever seen the movie The Hunger Games, you'll remember each district was focused on a single task: District 7 was the lumber district, District 8 focused on textile production, District 9 with grain etc.

District0x plans to do the same thing with the blockchain technology and Decentralized Autonomous Organizations (DAO). Each district will have its own payment and invoicing system, along with complete self governance. The venture will use the Ethereum blockchain to run smart contracts.

What District0x has done to make to the process user friendly, is combine different necessary (like smart contracts and payment processing) elements into a package, so it's not essential for users to completely understand the technology behind the platform. You can think of this as similar to how Wordpress works for web development. At the core of every district is the ability to operate a market or a bulletin board application.

Currently, there are over 100 district ideas in play. Theoretically, it would allow an individual such as you or me to implement their own version of AirBNB, Craigslist or Uber, without having to go through a middleman like the current system has to. This in turn reduces transaction fees and makes the overall cost lower for all parties involved. There are no fees to create districts, which makes them available to everyone. Currently, refundable deposits are required to put forward a district proposal, once the district passes quality control checks (ensuring the district is not there for malicious intent), the deposit is refunded to the district creator.

One such idea already running is Ethlance, an online freelancing platform similar to Upwork or Fiverr, but without the large transaction fees. Interestingly enough, the District0x team has actually hired developers via Ethlance to help them execute the project.

Another promising proposal is ShipIt, which focuses on the multi-billion dollar shipping industry. The idea is to create a decentralized maritime logistics platform. The sheer number of transactions in this industry alone (trucking, forwarding, warehousing etc.) make this a perfect foil for a blockchain solution.

The framework is in place, however the team needs to do more to gather traction, plus a larger user base to utilize their own districts. The current team is small, with just 10 members, plus an additional adviser, but there will certainly be additions in the future as the project continues to grow. Progress reports are frequent and developments are regular posted on GitHub.

One interesting approach the District0x team are employing is creating a free "education portal" to inform the wider public about the platform, and the real world functionality of districts. They are doing this are they believe the current limiting factor is a general ignorance of the potential of the platform. The portal is scheduled for rollout in Q4 2017.

District0x tokens (DNT) can be used to fund project and stake voting rights in different districts, the more tokens one has, the greater of a say they have. The one issue here is a possible abuse of a "pay to play" system.

The decentralized element of District0x means there is no single point of failure, for example there is no single server that all of the individual districts run from. This ensures that targeted hacking attacks cannot take down the entire network.

Supply wise, there are 600 million DNT available, with a total projected supply of 1 billion. It should be noted that in the white paper, the District0x team does reserve the right to add additional coins to the total supply, however this is contingent on the exchange rate between ETH/USD. For example, if ETH's value declines significantly vs. USD, the team can add additional coins to account for this fluctuation. This isn't necessarily something to be concerned about (financial hedging occurs all the time in fiat markets), but it's definitely something worth nothing.

Listing on larger exchanges will help spike the price in the short term. The team are in ongoing discussions with large exchange Bittrex, and a listing on there could easily see price rises of 100%. Long term prices will be largely determined by the number of popular districts that are set up using the platform. The next two planned district launches are Name Bazaar and Meme Factory.

Request Network (REQ)

Price at Time of Writing - $0.066

Market Cap at Time of Writing - $42,266,398

Available on:

BTC: Binance, Liqui

ETH: Binance, KuCoin, EtherDelta

Where to store: REQ is an ERC20 token so can be stored in MyEtherWallet

Request Network aims to become a decentralized payment network allowing both businesses and individuals to request money from anyone. The project aims to bring blockchain technology into the payment provider space, and act as competition to PayPal and Stripe. Request has already received industry plaudits as well as investment from US based startup investment group YCombinator.

Current centralized payment providers and networks take a commission of between 1.5% and 6% per transaction depending on the platform and the type of payment. Request Network aims to lower this fee to as little as 0.05% per transaction, with an average fee of 0.2% per transaction. This represents huge savings to the consumer and the merchant. Request also allows payment in cryptocurrency as well as fiat currency.

By utilizing Ethereum technology, all payments requested and made will be available on a public ledger for anyone to see. This level of transparency lowers the degree of fraudulent payments and fraudulent refund requests that currently plague traditional networks like PayPal and Stripe. This also has residual effects for areas like time sensitive money back guarantees or warranties for items.

Another advantage Request has versus traditional platforms is the transparency leads to lowering auditing costs. For example, in 2014 online Microsoft paid Deloitte over $45 million in auditing fees, and Bank of America paid over $100 million. With Request's public blockchain ledger, audits would effectively be carried out in real time and would represent a far less expensive option than hiring a third party to manual check that the transactions are valid.

Request Network is actually part of the 3,000 companies that are built on the Aragon testnet, which shows the interaction between blockchain projects. Request has also partnered with another blockchain project, Kyber, to improve the automatic currency conversion element of the platform. The Kyber partnership has great real world use potential as the merchant can specify payment in any cryptocurrency of their choosing, and the payee can still pay with their preferred cryptocurrency.

Request also recently introduced continuous payments, which allows users to be paid by the hour (and in theory, by the second). This is an ideal model for contractors or freelancers who work on an hourly basis rather than per project.

The team continues to deliver on the roadmap, with the latest update, known as "Colossus" being delivered ahead of schedule in Q4 2017 rather than the initially anticipated Q1 2018. Q1 2018 will see the "Great Wall" update, with a launch of Request Network on the Ethereum main net for the first time. The Great Wall update is of particular interest as this is when the "Pay with Request" button will be available to those who want to use it alongside traditional methods like "Pay with credit card" and "Pay with PayPal"

The payments sector is huge, and PayPal alone has an annual revenue of over $10 billion. If Request Network can capture even a small fraction of this, then there is potential for enormous growth. Alongside massive opportunity does come a certain amount of competition though, OmiseGO being the most well known one in the cryptocurrency space. There are also Populous and MetalPay, both of which have similar visions to Request.

A Low-Risk (But Still Highly Profitable) Way to Invest in Cryptocurrencies

For those of you familiar with traditional investments, then you'll likely to be aware of Exchange Traded Funds or ETFs. For those unfamiliar, and ETF is a security that trades like a regular stock, but instead of buying shares in one company, you are buying an aggregate of many companies. ETFs have an inherent advantage over single stocks in that by diversifying your risk over many companies, you are less likely to see sudden drops in price.

Based out of Slovenia, and active since November 2016, Fintech start-up Iconomi is currently running a blockchain based digital asset management platform using Ethereum technology. Known as Digital Asset Arrays (DAA), these are similar to ETFs and Index funds, as you are buying an aggregate of multiple cryptocurrencies instead of just one or two. Initial investments can be made with ETH or BTC, although there are plans to support fiat deposits in the coming months.

Their BLX blockchain index is the first passively managed array of digital assets, compromising of over 20 different cryptocurrencies, with the highest weight being in Bitcoin and Ethereum. The portfolio is re-balanced on a monthly basis, and different cryptocurrencies are added and removed based on performance. What's more is the BLX has currently outperformed both Ethereum and Litecoin over the past 6 months. There is also a more conservative fund which is composed of 60% Bitcoin, 20% Ethereum as well as 4 other ERC20 tokens. The fund have a 2-3% annual management fee, plus a 0.5% exit fee.

This could well be a good option if you're looking to invest in a multitude of cryptocurrencies, but don't want to deal with the hassle of signing up for multiple exchanges, and keeping track of various wallets. Iconomi currently offers 15 different DAAs, ranging from conservative, heavily Bitcoin based ones, to more risky ones featuring a multitude of smaller cap cryptocurrencies. Of course, like any investment, there are inherent risks involved, but if you're a more risk averse investor, who still wants to be a part of the cryptocurrency market, Iconomi is worth checking out.

Determinants of Cryptocurrency Growth Patterns in 2018 and Beyond

Coinbase

Regardless of your personal opinions on Coinbase as a cryptocurrency exchange, it still functions as the vast majority of user's first entry into the cryptocurrency market. It's accessibility and the ability to make purchases via debit and credit card means it's ideal as a "my first cryptocurrency exchange". Currently Coinbase allows the buying and selling of Bitcoin, Ethereum and Litecoin in exchange for fiat. However in November 2017, Coinbase announced that it would list ERC20 tokens in 2018, and any of the ERC20 below tokens being listed on Coinbase is sure to have a positive effect on price going forward. This also applies to other major exchanges such as Bitfinex and Bittrex, but Coinbase is the milestone here.

Market adoption

The later half of 2017 alone saw the cryptocurrency marketcap more than double to over $300 billion at the time of writing, and we are still very much in the infancy of cryptocurrency. Further investment by new players and a constant influx of new money into the market leads to bullish conditions. According to Forbes magazine, less than 0.5% of the world currently owns any form of cryptocurrency (and the vast majority of this will be Bitcoin).

We could look at this as a similar situation when the technology boom was in 1994, where email was the biggest use case, way before today's social media, video streaming, and online retail services. One could look at Bitcoin as the email of the cryptocurrency market. How does this relate to Ethereum? Well, in Ethereum's case, the vast majority of DApps aren't close to any sort of mass adoption, and it will likely be years before the market has matured.

Regulation

Regulation in various forms can have both positive and negative effects for the market as a whole. Ethereum itself was hit hard when headlines of "China bans ICOs" hit the front pages in late September. However, the news turned out to be temporary and the entire market recovered and surged in October and November. Large scale regulation in the US, China or Russia would indeed have a negative impact on both price and the technology future of Ethereum based projects.

Neo

Neo is the cryptocurrency project most similar to Ethereum in terms of being a platform that other blockchain companies can build on top of. Ethereum has a much wider adoption currently, but Neo is based out of China, and following on from the above point - Chinese government regulation in favor of a "domestic coin" could hurt Ethereum's adoption potential in the Chinese market. For example, an announcement that all Chinese ICOs must be built using Neo is plausible, and as China represents a large part of the cryptocurrency market, this will in turn have a negative effect on Ethereum. That being said, the above is an extreme scenario, and there is no reason that Ethereum and Neo cannot co-exist.

Futures Market & Institutional Investing

Institutional investors will play a big part in the growth of Ethereum as a tradable asset, and the release of an Ethereum futures market, where traders can bet the future price of Ethereum, will signify that it is maturing. As of yet, only Bitcoin futures can be traded, but as Ethereum matures more as an asset, there is no doubt that a similar market for trading ETH will emerge.

Moving to Proof of Stake

One of the largest technological challenges surrounding Ethereum is the move from a Proof of Work (PoW) mining algorithm to a more environmentally friendly Proof of Stake (PoS) one. The original PoW method is similar to the one used by Bitcoin, in that computers solve cryptographic puzzles (or complex mathematical equations) in order to validate a transaction and create a block. This method requires increasing amounts of computing power to mine cryptocurrency, and can leads to issues such as the vast majority of the mining power being concentrated in the hands of just a few miners (for example, someone running a large scale mining operation). It is this kind of centralization that Ethereum seeks to avoid. There is also the issue of electricity use, both Ethereum and Bitcoin are currently estimated to use over $1 million worth of electricity *per day* in their mining process, which is more electricity than a moderately sized country than Ireland or Denmark.

A PoS mining algorithm differs because it allows holders of ETH to deposit or "stake" their coins in order to validate the next block. The public blockchain tracks who holds ETH, and how much of it they have staked. Therefore, you don't need expensive hardware to participate in the mining process. Mining rewards are proportional to how much you have staked, so someone staking 10 ETH would get 10x the rewards of someone staking 1 ETH. PoS also has the advantage of shortening network transaction times, and making them more consistent. So instead of an average transaction time of 15 per second, the 15 transactions confirmed every second, like clockwork. PoS also allows ETH to be used as an asset and could be looked at like a savings account, because if you staked your ETH on the a network, you would essentially receive interest from mining rewards.

Ethereum's initial move will be to a Hybrid PoW/PoS algorithm in the "Casper" update to the platform. At the time of writing, the Casper update is live on the Ethereum TestNet, so the code isn't finalized but it can be tested for security and safety issues.

A full move to PoS is scheduled in Q1/Q2 2018 in the "Metropolis" update. A smooth transition to PoS will leads to a fairer Ethereum mining ecosystem in the long run, but like any big transition of this kind, there are challenges in the execution. Naturally, any safety or security breaches will lead to negative results for Ethereum, as will technical issues such as users not being able to stake their ETH. As the technology is still very much in it infant stages, these are the kinds of areas that we must be extra cautious of when considered investing.

Adoption in Asia

In June of 2017, South Korea overtook the US and China as the largest Ethereum market in terms of daily trading volume. Roughly $200 million of Ethereum is traded everyday on BitHumb, Korea's largest cryptocurrency exchange. Continued adoption in Asia is part of Ethereum's growth plan for 2018 and beyond, with a Chinese office opening next year, and a growing number of partnerships with Chinese companies in the works.

Conclusion

Ethereum has changed the way we look at financial transactions, auditing and the idea of a middleman. Our previous reliance on banks and other financial institutions has been put into question, and we are now moving forward towards a dcentralized financial world. These multibillion dollar corporations and industries are facing disruption, and actual competition, for the first time in over a century.

For consumers, cross border payments at a near-instant transaction time, and far lower transactions fees are making the global economy smaller and more accessible.

Beyond Ethereum, blockchain technology has an additional laundry list of benefits ranging from transparency in elections to easily accessible medical records between parties.

As a commodity, no other financial asset, cryptocurrency or otherwise has produced better returns for investors over the past 12 months.

For those who believe in Ethereum, and Vitalik Buterin's vision for a better world, long may these returns continue.

I hope you've enjoyed this book and that you're now a little bit more informed about how Ethereum works, and more importantly, how it can work for you. Whether you're planning on investing for the long-term - I wish you the best of luck.

Remember, trade rationally and not emotionally. Never invest more than you can afford to lose, and for the love of God - don't check the charts 15 times a day.

Now, if you're ready to make the next step and get involved in the market. I have a small gift for you.

If you sign up for Coinbase using this link, you will receive $10 worth of free Bitcoin after your first purchase of more than $100 worth of cryptocurrency.

Cryptocurrency: Mining for Beginners - How You Can Make Up To $18,500 a Year Mining Coins From Home

By Stephen Satoshi

Introduction

Welcome to the exciting world of cryptocurrency mining. First things first, congratulations on buying this book and thank you for doing so.

The following chapters will discuss in detail what exactly cryptocurrency mining is, how it works, and most importantly, different ways you can make a profit from mining cryptocurrency.

You'll learn about various mining techniques such as staking, pool mining, and rig mining. You'll also discover "outside the box" ways to profit from mining coins, some of which don't even require you to do any mining yourself. Of course, as is the case with all my books, we'll also be highlighting any cryptocurrency scams or schemes which I feel you should avoid as well.

These are truly exciting ways of earning coins without having to buy at the exchanges.

Finally, this book assumes you have little to no knowledge of cryptocurrency mining and how it all works, so the language is designed to be as easy to understand as possible.

I hope you enjoy the content of this book, and I wish you the best of your cryptocurrency journey.

Thanks,

Stephen

Basic Overview of Mining Cryptocurrencies

By now you probably already know a decent amount about cryptocurrencies. They are digital assets that function as a medium of exchange and use cryptography to secure transactions and to create additional units. Cryptocurrencies are mined into existence through a process known as mining. This process of mining new cryptocurrencies involves two functions. These are adding transactions to the blockchain and releasing new currency to the system.

Mining Cryptocurrencies

In order to mine cryptocurrencies, you need access to a powerful computer and special software. There are new, sophisticated computers in the market that have been developed specifically for cryptocurrency mining.

A miner is basically anyone who invests his or her time confirming cryptocurrency transactions and adding new currencies to its network. Mining cryptocurrency requires plenty of resources. The computers needed for this process are costly and operating costs are very high. This is because the mining process consumes a lot of electricity.

Miners generally spend most of their time trying to confirm a block containing data using hash functions. To understand better how the mining process works, it is important to first understand the basic aspects of blockchain technology.

Mining and the Blockchain

Cryptocurrencies use publicly distributed and decentralized ledgers known as blockchain. Blockchains are secure networks and this is in part due to the mining process. Mining is, therefore, an essential component of the blockchain and is integral to its stability. It provides an additional level of security because the process validates each transaction that takes place on the blockchain.

In fact, the validity of each cryptocurrency coin is secured by the blockchain. Each block contains what is known as a hash pointer. The blockchain is decentralized with no central server to log in all transactions. However, without sufficient computing power, the blockchain ledger cannot operate. Cryptocurrencies rely on the combined power of numerous mining computers spread out across the world.

These computers are operated by miners who lend their computers for a common cause. In return for their input, they receive an incentive or reward. Miners receive payment when they solve a challenging mathematical puzzle and validate transactions before others do.

Each block in the blockchain contains transaction data, a timestamp, and a hash pointer.

Hash Function

The hash function in cryptocurrency is an algorithm that maps data of varying or arbitrary size to a hash and is by design a one-way function. A hash pointer is present in all block and always points to the previous block. It acts as a pointer, making it easy to track transactions.

Proof of Work

Most of the blockchains in use today use a concept known as Proof of Work. Proof of Work protocol or system is simply an economic measure that requires some work from the requesters to be done. This work is often processing time by a computer. This helps prevent service abuse.

Proof of Work scheme is the first timestamping scheme that was invented for the blockchain. The most popular proof-of-work schemes are based on scrypt and SHA-256. Scrypt is the most widely used among cryptocurrencies. Others include SHA-3, Crypto-Night and Blake.

CPU versus GPU Mining

There are several options available when it comes to cryptocurrency mining. At the onset of cryptocurrencies, you could effectively run the mining algorithms on your computer as an individual miner. The regular computer at your home or office operates on a CPU or central processing unit which was powerful enough to handle mining functions.

Mining at the onset simply meant downloading or compiling the correct mining software and the wallet for a preferred coin. A miner would then configure the mining software to join their preferred cryptocurrency network then dedicate your computer to the task of mining cryptocurrencies.

In recent months and years, miners turned from CPU computers to GPU-based PCs. The GPU is the graphics processing unit that processes video systems on your computer. Basically, a GPU is like a CPU but a lot more powerful and designed to execute specific tasks. It is this specialization that makes the GPU suited for tasks such as cryptocurrency mining.

Compare CPU vs. GPU Capacity

A CPU core can execute only 4 or 32-bit instructions per clock while a GPU can execute 32—32-bit instructions in the same period of time. This simply means a GPU processor executes 800 times more instructions per clock.

Even though the latest, most modern CPUs have even 12 cores and much higher frequency clocks, still one GPU, like the HD5970, is more than 5 times faster than 4 modern CPUs combined. Therefore, GPU mining can result in faster transaction times and you can gain more coins in the same time frame.

Functions of the GPU versus the CPU

The CPU is the executive arm of the computer. The central processing unit is essentially a decision maker that is directed by the software in use. CPUs do all sorts of mathematical computations. On the other hand, a GPU is more of a laborer than an executive. GPUs contain large numbers of ALUs, or arithmetic and logic units. This makes them capable of executing large quantities of bulky mathematical labor in a greater quantity than CPUs.

What you need to be concerned with is the fact that the advent of GPU mining has made CPU mining almost obsolete. This is because the hash rate of most cryptocurrency networks increased exponentially. CPU mining is hardly profitable on some cryptocurrency networks but is thriving on others. It has largely been affected by the increased hash rate.

GPU mining is significantly faster in comparison and hence profitable on all cryptocurrency systems. Today, cryptocurrency mining heavily relies on GPU-based mining rigs. A mining rig is a computer system or arrangement that is used for mining coins. Most rigs are dedicated to accomplishing only one task, which in this case, is crypto mining.

Buying GPUs

When it comes to considering specific graphics cards for your mining rig, the first choice for many miners is the NVIDIA GeForce 1080 Ti which provides the greatest overall hashing power of any GPU on the market, though it is also known to consume more power when under a full mining load than any other GPU as well.

The more midrange option is currently the GTX 1070 or the AMD Radeon RX 480 for a more balanced mix of performance and power consumption. In fact, with the proper modifications, the GTX 1070 can generate performance that is nearly on par with the 1080 Ti while still consuming significantly less power overall.

While the popularity of cryptocurrency mining means that the market for GPUs is occasionally hit with artificial market scarcity as miners buy up the whole supply as soon as it is released, you should typically be able to find a GTX 1070 for under $500. When they are hard to find, however, you can easily see the price skyrocket to $700 or more. If you find that the prices you are seeing are in this upper range, then you will likely want to keep a close eye on Amazon for when a new shipment hits the market as you will then be more likely to find it at the traditional MSRP.

With the GTX 1070 in hand, you can then make use of a program known as MSI Afterburner to increase the memory interface clock to 650 MHz and reduce the power target to 66 percent to decrease heat output and board power consumption as much as possible. This, in turn, will ensure that GPU temperatures remain around a reasonable 66 degrees Celsius which is nearly 15 degrees cooler than what it would be running at without the tweaks. This, in turn, raises the average hash rate from 27.24 MH/s to 31.77 MH/s. With this hashing power, combined with an average power consumption of 177 and a cost per kilowatt hour at 10 cents, you are looking at a profit of about $140 per month.

Proof of Work vs. Proof of Stake

Proof of Work was designed as a protocol to achieve consensus and deter or prevent cyber attacks, especially distributed denial-of-service or DDoS. Such attacks have the sole purpose of diminishing or even exhausting the resources of computer systems through repeated sending of fake requests.

Proof of Work concept has been around for many years, way before cryptocurrencies. Today, it is adopted by different cryptocurrency systems such as Ethereum, Bitcoin, and Litecoin because it allows distributed consensus across systems. It is used mainly to create decentralized agreements about adding blocks to the network between different computers or nodes within the network.

HashCash is an example of Proof of Work function used by Bitcoin. Bitcoin miners spend a lot of time mining the currency. For a block to be added to the network, HashCash needs to produce very specific data that will verify the amount of work that goes into producing the currency.

Proof of Work is Integral to Crypto Mining

Being the traditional mining method many of the older cryptocurrencies use, Proof of Work has become an essential requirement when mining cryptocurrencies.   When cryptos are mined, miners verify transactions on blocks are legitimate. In order for the verification to happen, miners have to solve a complex mathematical problem. This problem is also known as the proof-of-work problem.

One thing to note is that as the network increases in size and the coins gain in value, the problems become increasingly harder to solve. Therefore more computational power is required as we move forward, I discuss this in greater depth in the chapter "Why I don't recommend you mine Bitcoin".

Proof of Stake

Another aspect that is commonplace with crypto mining is Proof of Stake. Proof of stake is another different method of validating crypto transactions. It is an algorithm that produces the same result as Proof of Work but using a different process. Proof of Stake came much later and was first used in 2012.

While Proof of Work algorithm compensates miners who solve mathematical problems, Proof of Stake identifies miners using a different approach. On the Proof of Stake protocol, there is no block reward. This is because digital currencies using this system are pre-mined and their number does not change. Since there is no block reward, miners are paid a transaction fee and are referred to as forgers instead.

Benefits of Proof of Stake over Proof of Work

- Validators do not have to use any computing power.

- It saves validators a lot of money in energy costs.

- Proof of Stake ensures a safer network.

- It makes attacks very costly because those doing the attacking must own a significant proportion of the coins themselves. Therefore they are essentially attacking their own coins. It would be like robbers deciding to rob a bank they owned 51% of.

Why I Don't Recommend You Mine Bitcoin

Whenever Bitcoin's price is rising (and that's most of the time!), the mining question always pops up. Usually from those who are inexperienced or want a "free" way to get a piece of the pie.

It all starts with a variant of this question.

"Why buy Bitcoin at $100/$1,000/$4,000 when you can just use your computer to mine some for free?"

Unfortunately, like everything else - there is no such thing as free Bitcoin.

As previously discussed, the way Bitcoin is created or "mined" is by using a computer to solve an of increasingly complex series of algorithms. Users are then rewarded for solving these algorithms by receiving Bitcoin. There is no man power involved, you yourself don't have to solve the algorithm, you just have to link your computer up to the Bitcoin network and the computer does the rest. There are also no shortcuts or breakthrough moments, the only way Bitcoin can be obtained quicker is with more computer power. How much computational power you supply determines the size of your reward. The more power you supply, the more Bitcoins you receive.

Now here is why mining is generally a terrible investment for the average Joe.

1. Electricity Costs - The electricity costs involved with running your computer 24/7 (which is necessary for mining) by far outweigh the amount of Bitcoins you receive for completing the task. You require access to industrial electricity rates of around $0.02 per kWh in order for the venture to be profitable on a small scale. The vast majority of people cannot access these rates without some sort of special connection.

2. Requiring Specialist Hardware - Nowadays, the most efficient mining processes require special hardware known as Application-specific integrated circuits (ASIC). ASICs can be described as a supercomputer that can only ever perform one task. Specialist Bitcoin ASIC miners available for consumer purchase still start at around $1000 and often run around $2000-$2500.

3. Equipment maintenance - To maintain all this computing power is an additional cost. The cost of cooling alone is a large cost that has to be factored into long term profits. Hardware running 24/7 burns out faster and replacement mining equipment will be needed in due course.

4. The increasing size of the Bitcoin network - The network pays out a fixed amount of Bitcoin, regardless of how many miners are using the network. The current rate is around 1800BTC per day, which sounds like a huge number until you realize just how many miners there are on the network. The current mining power is equivalent to 17.6 BILLION desktop computers. Therefore the average payout for the end user running 1 desktop computer, with a standard, not designed for mining GPU, full time is approximately $0.000107 per day. Or roughly 2 cents a year's worth of BTC. To put it lightly, you have more chance of winning the lottery than you do making a profit from mining Bitcoin your standard home computer.

Mining in 2017 is a much different proposition from mining in 2010 or even 2012. There are some opportunities which involved investing in Bitcoin farms or group purchasing processing power of ASIC at a discount. This is known as a "mining pool". Due to cheaper power costs currently around 80% of the world's mining pools are based in China, with Iceland possessing the second largest number. Joining a mining pool requires a lower upfront investment but still requires cheap electricity rates and have debatable ROI potential.

It should also be worth noting that many of those who promote group mining or cloud mining do so under an affiliate program with whatever company that is promoting, meaning they get a commission % every time someone signs up.

However, for the average Joe without a huge amount of money to invest - I would strongly recommend buying coins instead of mining them. You are more likely to get higher returns in both the short and long run.

Ethereum Mining & Switch to Proof of Stake

Ethereum is one of the most popular cryptocurrencies on the market today and is second only to Bitcoin in terms of popularity and market capitalization. Ethereum mining is the process of mining Ether, the token used on this cryptocurrency system. Ether provides the only pathway of using this powerful network.

Ether mining does not just increase ether volumes but also helps secure the network. When ether is mined, it creates, verifies, propagates, and publishes blocks on the blockchain. We can conclude, therefore, that mining ether also secures the network and ensures transactions are verified.

There are major organizations and developers running smart contracts on Ethereum network. In fact, ether is looked at as an incentive to motivate developers who wish to create powerful applications.

Essentially, a developer has to mine ether which will be used on the network or sold to interested buyers later. Executing transactions on Ethereum network is a much cheaper method of using the network compared to buying ether directly.

How Ethereum Mining Works

Ethereum mining is very similar to Bitcoin mining. For each block of transactions, miners have to repeatedly compute and come up with a solution to a complex mathematical puzzle. In other words, Ethereum miners have to run a block's unique metadata through a hash function. The metadata includes software version and timestamp.

The hash then returns a scrambled, fixed length string of letters and numbers. Only the nonce value changes which in turn affects the resulting hash value. When a miner finds the hash that matches the current target, he or she will be rewarded with ether and the entire blockchain will be updated with this information.

If you are mining a particular block but another miner finds its hash, then you will have to cease work on that block and begin working on the next block. It is almost impossible for anyone to cheat at crypto mining. You cannot fake the work and then emerge with the correct solution to the puzzle. This is why they use Proof of Work protocol to secure the network. However, verifying transactions takes almost no time.

Miners find a block approximately every 12 to 15 seconds. Should this speed get faster or slow down, then the Ethereum algorithm will automatically reset the difficulty level of the mathematical puzzle. The readjustments of the difficulty level are meant to maintain the solution time at 12 – 15 seconds.

Mining profitability depends a lot on luck and the amount of computing power devoted to the mining process.

Ether mostly uses a Proof of Work algorithm known as Ethash. Ethash demands more memory so that it is difficult to mine using these costly ASIC computers which are specialized computers with advanced processors that are largely used to mine Bitcoin. This is probably why there are no ASICs specifically designed for mining ether.

Even then, Ethereum mining will not go on forever. The network is transitioning from Proof of Work to Proof of Stake. Proof of Work essentially protects the network from tampering and determines which transactions are valid. On the other hand, proof of stake is where stakeholders secure the network through their own tokens.

How to Start Mining Ethereum

The process of mining is considered as the glue that holds the entire Ethereum network together. It achieves this by engaging in consensus on any changes that take place on the applications running on the network.

As a miner, you need to add your computer to a node in the network to join others trying to solve complex mathematical puzzles. You need to try a large number of mathematical problems until one of them gets solved and releases new ether.

Joining the Network

In theory, anyone with a computer can join the Ethereum network and begin mining coins. However, as more and more miners join, the blockchain requires more and more power so that joining now requires a very powerful computer. To be successful, you will need a high-powered computer with the appropriate mining software.

Find Appropriate Mining Hardware

As you already know by now, to mine ether, you require specialized computer hardware that will be dedicated to full-time computer mining. Ideally, you can choose between CPU or GPU mining hardware. However, as of today, CPUs have become almost a novelty and only GPU hardware is available, especially for Ethereum mining.

There are plenty of GPU computers in the market and setting up one is not a simple task. First find out which particular models are the most profitable based on parameters such as power consumption, hash rate performance and cost. It is advisable to set up a mining rig. A mining rig is simply a system of GPU computers assembled together. Such a rig might take you up to a week to set up.

You should work out your profitability, so you know how much profit you will be making. There are mining calculators available that can help you compute your expected profitability. The most accurate one right now can be found at CryptoCompare.com/mining

The results will let you know how much ether you will earn at a particular hash rate.

Ethereum's Switch from Proof of Work to Proof of Stake Protocols

Ethereum is expected to make its biggest upgrade ever. According to its inventor, Vitalik Buterin, Ethereum will move from use of Proof of Concept to Proof of Stake. The switch and adoption is expected to end in about one year's time.

Ethereum is expected to achieve this move by implementing the software known as Casper. Casper v1 is a hybrid of Proof of Work and Proof of Sale concepts. This software is going to decrease and finally end the use of Proof of Concept. This essentially means that Ethereum mining will no longer be profitable.

What is Casper?

Casper is a Proof of Stake algorithm that will start running on the Ethereum network this year (2018). The first version of the software is a hybrid of both Proof of Concept and Proof of Stake. However, it is expected that Proof of Concept consensus will eventually be eliminated so a lot of the power that miners currently have will be removed. Also, Proof of Stake algorithm uses far less energy to operate the network. It offers additional protection such as reduced centralization and preventing 51% attacks.

The Ethereum community believes that this switch will help address the problem of scalability that the network is currently facing. Casper will allow the network to scale more efficiently and also enable new blocks to be created faster and added to the network. Scalability will be managed through a process known as sharding. Sharding is the process of partitioning a large database horizontally into smaller and easily managed parts.

Benefits of Shift from PoW to PoS

The Network will not consume as much power as is currently the case. It is estimated that both Ethereum and Bitcoin consume $1 million worth of energy and hardware per day just to keep the networks up and running.

The network will not need to issue as many coins as it currently does in order to motivate participants to keep operating within the network. PoS will discourage the formation of centralized cartels that may cause harm to the network. The 51% attacks will be minimized as economic penalties can be used to make the attacks very costly.

Will Miners be Affected by this Shift?

The profitability of mining on the Ethereum network will definitely be affected. Miners will not earn as much as they currently do. The complete shift to PoS is expected to take between one and two years so there is no immediate effect on current miners.

The Ethereum community has agreed to this shift so it will happen. Starting 2018, the reward from a single block will decrease from 5 ether to 3 ether. Miners can start mining other coins such as Ethereum Classic or Monero.

To understand why this change could be so huge for Ethereum, it is important to understand just how it differs from the proof of work model. With a proof of stake verification system, instead of having the miner solve the equation in order to verify the block, a validator, who is confirmed reliable by the stake they have in the system, will commit to its accuracy, knowing that if they lie they will lose their own ether as well. The Alliance is currently testing the new system through a limited use verification process to make sure it is ready for a wider launch soon.

This will ultimately serve to make mining more egalitarian as a whole as it will no longer be based around who has the best mining machine, thus leveling the playing field as all the mining will be done on the blockchain itself. It will also serve to make 51 percent attacks more difficult to pull off as it requires direct contact with other miners as opposed to just having enough hardware to brute force the blockchain successfully.

Mining Versus Buying Cryptocurrencies

At this point, you're probably wondering if it is more profitable to buy coins than to mine them. Answering this question is not easy as there are many factors which affect the final outcome. However, it is possible to examine the two and come up with a reasonable conclusion. The question is if you had $10,000, would it be better to invest it in a mining operation or just buy coins?

Cloud Mining for Cryptocurrencies

Let us first try and understand different mining operations. Cloud mining has become rather popular in the recent past because it enables small investors to pool resources and participate in crypto mining. There are a number of companies that provide credible cloud mining services.

Cloud mining is a service that offers you an opportunity to invest a small amount of money and participate in the mining of a given cryptocurrency. What you are doing by joining such an operation is essentially to rent crypto mining hardware and receive a share of the mined coins in return.

As a participant in a cloud mining operation, you will be paying for a given hash rate for a set period of time. For instances, you can rent 10 THS for a 3-year period to mine Ethereum. Sometimes your contractual obligations may require that you pay for some expenses such as electricity and maintenance. These are often charged on a daily basis but billed weekly or monthly.

Pros and Cons of Cloud Mining

Pros

- As an investor, you do not need to invest in actual equipment. Crypto mining equipment can be quite expensive, especially high-end hardware.

- Setting up mining equipment can be tricky and time consuming. It can take up to one week just setting up a series of powerful crypto mining hardware. Fortunately, cloud mining members do not have to worry about equipment setup or even monitoring and maintenance.

- There is no need to worry about electricity things such as the noise and heat generated by the mining operation.

- You are also able to invest a relatively small amount of money in such a major operation and earn handsome returns. If done well, crypto mining can be a source of additional revenue and sometimes even your main source of income.

Cons

- As an investor in a cloud mining operation, you do not own any of the hardware or other equipment used in the operation. As such, you are left with no hardware at the end of your contract even though any money you paid upfront will not be returned.

- Sometimes it costs a lot more to join a cloud mining operation especially if you want a higher hash rate for a higher return on investment.

- You are not guaranteed that the cloud mining company will be there at the end of your contract. There is a certain level of risk involved here.

Crypto Buying versus Mining

To find out which one, between mining and buying, is more profitable, we need to find out how much we can make using either process by investing $10,000. At today's rate of 1BTC=$8,240 (as of Feb 7th, 2017), our $10,000 will fetch about 1.21 BTC. You can check the latest rates at sites such as www.CoinLlama.com.

Now we need to see if we can make more money than this through mining. It is never an easy thing working out profitability because of the many factors at play. Some of the variables involved include increasing mining difficulty and energy costs.

Find the Best Crypto Mining Equipment

Now since most of the $10,000 will be spent buying equipment, it is advisable to find the best in the market. The main issue you are likely to face is that most credible mining products are often out of stock and so you may have to create a pre-order. However, if you search harder, you are likely to find excellent products. You can check out companies like Butterfly Labs or Bit-Main.

Calculate the Amount of Crypto You Can Mine with $10,000

You can easily find a Bitcoin mining calculator online which you can use for this purpose. Even then, there are some variables that still remain unknown and you will have to work with estimates. One of these variables is the rate at which the mining difficulty will increase while the other is the exchange rate of Bitcoin with time.

The equipment you need might cost something like $8000. This is the cost of about 7 Antminer S4-B2 miners. You do not have to host the computers at home or in your office. Instead, you can have them hosted in China where hosting and energy costs are quite low. These machines are also quite noisy and generate plenty of heat. The rest of the costs including shipping, daily hosting, and electricity amount to a little over 9,200. The balance can pay for electricity and hosting costs for a period of about three months. Daily expenses are roughly around $7.2.

Now, most calculators show that you are likely to make just about the same amount of crypto initially invested. This means that, in some instances, buying and mining coins add up to almost the same amount.

Ethereum Mining versus Buying

Ethereum mining seems to be a lot more profitable than buying. Take the example of tech researchers who invested 1500 Euros in a mining operation and another 1500 Euros buying ether. They mining rig was mining Ethereum at 147 MH/s. This was a real experiment that was conducted starting June 2016.

Outcomes

The 1500 Euros bought 136 ETH or ether tokens. However, after 6 months, the mining rig had generated almost 105 ETH. By the end of March 2016, the researchers had mined over 140 ETH. By June of 2017, the mining operation had earned about 152 ETH compared to the 136 initially purchased.

In both operations, it seems like mining has an edge over buying. This is true because you can continue mining coins for a long time, recover your initial investment, and continue making money.

The only downside is that machines do break down with time, hash rates change, and conditions in the crypto mining sector hardly remain the same. There are always policy changes and so on.

In conclusion, if you want to make instant money, then invest in cryptocurrencies, subject to performance in the market. However, for long term investment, then mining may well be the better of the two options.

How to Setup your Own Mining Rig

Building your own cryptocurrency mining rig is more like growing your own money tree. You will create wealth in the form of cryptocurrencies even as you go about your daily business.

What is a mining rig? A mining rig refers to a system of computers that are set up together for purposes of mining cryptocurrencies such as Ethereum or Bitcoin. Mining is the process of extracting crypto tokens from a blockchain network.

A mining rig can be dedicated, which means it has been constructed and set up specifically to mine cryptocurrencies. The rig can also be a system of computers that have the capacity to mine crypto coins.

Setting up a Rig

Setting up a mining rig is a two-step process. First, you will have to identify the equipment that you need. Choosing and sourcing the right equipment for your preferred mining operation. The second step involves putting the equipment together. Putting the rig together is a technical process that is similar but more complex to building your own computer.

Mining rigs consist of similar components found in most desktop computers. However, there are a couple of differences. For instance, in your regular desktop computer, there is a general balance between components such as HD, GPU, RAM, and CPU. With mining rigs, you want a very basic HD, bare minimum RAM memory, the lowest clocked CPU and 5 – 7 GPUs. It is not possible to fit this kind of equipment in a normal computer case, so you will most likely need a custom-made case that will hold all your equipment.

How to Pick the Correct Mining Rig Parts

GPU Mining Cards

GPU stands for graphics processing units. When it comes to GPUs, you want to select the very best in the market. Basically, search for GPUs with low power usage, low cost, and a high hash rate. It's easier to start with just one GPU then scale up to 5 or 6. Anything beyond 7 will be difficult to stabilize. You should aim to find a balance between a GPU with low power consumption and the highest hash rate. The hash rate denotes the speed at which it can mine cryptocurrencies. There is quite a variety of GPUs to choose from, depending on the currency that you intend to mine. Make sure you do not buy your GPUs or any other components off a street corner because they often have problems that you won't notice until you get home and plug in the card. However, you can find good quality, second hand processors at reputable outlets.

Mining Rig Case

As already noted above, crypto mining rigs cannot fit in regular computer cases. You will need to either buy a custom-made case or build your own. You can easily build your own case at home. Most miners do so using either plastic storage crates or a milk case. They both function really well even though they may not look that great. You can even choose to create a wooden case if you wish. It's really all up to you, aesthetics are not our main focus here.

Power Supply

The standard desktop computer uses a standard power supply ranging from 300W – 500W. When it comes to a mining rig, you will require a lot more power. If you create a mining rig with 6 to 7 GPUs, you need to ensure that you have access to sufficient power. You should have access to at least 1,200W. The supply efficiency should be certified at Gold or better. Make sure that the power supply is modular so that you configure your cables individually. This will turn out to be extremely important when building your rig.

A Motherboard

A motherboard is essential the brain of your computer and forms the base of your mining rig. It is on the motherboard that you build everything. When searching for one, you will be looking to find one with sufficient GPU slots because these will determine the number of GPUs or graphics card that can be accommodated. The number of GPUs will also determine, in the end, your total hash power. Most GPUs work on a PCI express so find a motherboard with at least 3 PCI Express slots. You can fit 3 GPUs on this motherboard each with a hash rate of 20 MH/s so that in total you have 60 MH/s. You can also opt for CPU-Motherboard combinations which are readily available. For purposes of coin mining, you will have to maximize the number of GPUs that your motherboard can support. Find one that can accommodate between 6 and 7 GPUs. Such motherboards are hard to find in stores, so you may want to search for them online. Great examples include the ASUS Prime Z270-P Motherboard or the Intel Celeron G3930.

Powered Riser Cables

Also crucial for your mining rig are powered riser cables. You will need these to extend PCI-e connections from the motherboard. This way, you will be able to mount the GPUs within your crate, or case. You should find as many PCI cables as you can and ensure that they match up with the total number of GPUs that you have.

Hard Drive

You will require a suitable hard drive where you will store your mining software and operating system. A good, solid state drive will do just fine. SSD hard drives are so called because they do not have any moving parts which can break or give in. the size will basically depend on what things you will do when mining so take that into consideration. For instance, if you need to download the entire blockchain, then you will need a sizeable hard drive to store the blockchain. However, if you have no such intentions, then a standard, 120 GB SSD will do.

The Operating System

Linux has some of the most powerful operating systems capable of mining multiple coins such as Monero, Z-cash, and Ethereum. There are also Window's based mining operating systems. Some are specific such as the Eth OS which is the operating system that mines Ethereum on Linux. There are a couple of others to choose from so ensure that you choose the correct one for whichever coin you are focusing on.

Accessories and Other Essential Components

You will also require additional components for your mining rig. These include RAM memory, a basic monitor and mouse, and a couple of box fans. Get a single fan for each separate rig. For the RAM, you will need a single 4GB 1600MHz and nothing more.

Put the Mining Rig Together

Now that you have all the components with you, you need to put it all together. If you have experience building a PC, then this will not be much different. You will probably find it easy. However, anyone can learn how to assemble a mining rig.

Crypto Wallet

First things first, you will need a cryptocurrency wallet. The wallet will store the coins you mine. You will want to get a reliable hardware wallet such as the Ledger Nano S. This wallet is immune to viral and malware attacks and just cannot be hacked.

The monitor will provide you with additional security because it displays crucial wallet details. You can use the Ledger Nano S to store Bitcoins, Litecoin, Z-cash, Dash, DodgeCoin, and Ethereum.

How to Put it All Together

First, confirm that your power supply unit is able to handle the GPU cards in your system. Also, ensure that your riser cables can reach your additional GPUs within your rig. The GPUs should be safely located and secured. So, set up the GPUs and ensure they are well distributed. Remember that GPUs do get quite hot and they generate plenty of heat. Place the GPUs in a well-ventilated room. Also, ensure that your rig is mining once it is set up.

First install the operating system, followed by the mining software onto your PC. You can choose either Ubuntu from Linux or Windows from Microsoft. Windows is preferable because it has automated the installation of drivers. This enables all components within your computer to communicate and interact easily. However, Ubuntu is free and offers you more options.

Once the GPUs have been set up and attached to the motherboard, you will need to check that everything else is in place. For instance, are the fans available to cool the GPUs? Once everything is setup, you can test the equipment and then proceed to mine your preferred cryptocurrency. If you want to mine

Ethereum, then you can download EthOs. This is an APP specifically designed for mining Ethereum. While it is advisable to have this APP, it is not essential and you can do without it.

Beginning Mining

Now that your equipment is all set up, you can then begin the mining process. There are two different approaches that you can use. These are solo mining and pool mining.

Solo mining: As a solo miner, you will be working against the other miners because you will be competing to mine ether. If you rig is able to generate the correct hash, then you earn the block reward. If you have a rig of 60 MH/s against the network's 1.2 GH, you will not earn ether as often as you would want. You may also have to download the entire blockchain. You will need sufficient memory space for this.

Pool mining: This is a crypto mining process where you join other miners and team up in order to minimize the volatility of your earnings. This way, you will be able to earn ether every day due to increased hash power. The reward you get on a regular basis will be equivalent to the amount of work your system puts in. You will also not have to download the entire blockchain onto your computer.

You can choose to join programs such as Miner Gate for more efficient pool mining. Miner Gate allows its members to mine coins via options. You can also mine two different currencies at the same time and without losing any hash rate that is geared towards your main currency. However, Miner Gate is not the only option you have, and you can still join other less sophisticated mining pools.

Equipment Cost

Mining equipment is not cheap especially the latest models which are specifically designed for crypto mining. It should be noted, all these ROI figures are just an estimate based on the prices at the time of writing. Actual returns figures will vary.

L3+ Antminer ASIC: This mining equipment costs about $1580 on average. It has a hash rate of 504 MH/s and can bring in a return of about $5.15 per day. You can expect a payback on your investment in 305 days.

Bitmain Antminer S9: One of the best pieces of mining equipment is the Antminer S9. It is designed to mine Bitcoin and is a very costly piece of equipment. It costs $6,600 at Amazon and has an impressive hash rate of 14 TH/s.

Bitmain Antminer S7: The Antminer S7 from Bitmain costs $1,400. It comes with a hard disk of 512 MB, SD-RAM memory and operates on a Linux platform.

Antminer Power Supply: The power supply for the Antminer costs $170. Second hand versions are much cheaper, costing about $130.

What is Cloud Mining?

Cloud mining can be described as the process of mining cryptos via a remote data center where mining power is shared among members. Such arrangements enable interested members to join the cloud and participate in coin mining operations without the need to buy or manage the hardware.

In cloud mining operations, mining rigs are located and maintained within a facility owned or rented by a mining company. Members simply need to register and purchase shares or mining contracts in return for a share of the mining rewards. However, there are weekly or monthly costs such as overheads, rent, and electricity costs that have to be paid. This amount is normally deducted from the earnings of the cloud members.

Therefore, if you want to invest in coin mining operations without the trouble of buying and managing your own hardware, there is an alternative in cloud mining. By joining a could mining operation, you get to share processing power with other remote miners. All you need to join a cloud is your own computer for communication purposes, a wallet to receive your pay and payment required for sign up.

Different Types of Hosting

Companies providing cloud mining services can either lease a virtual private server or a physical mining server then install mining software. Sometimes these companies opt for hashing power hosted at a data center instead of leasing dedicated servers. Hashing power is normally denominated in GH/s or GigaHash per second. The contracts signed often indicate the period for the contract and desired hashing power.

Pros of Cloud Mining

- Mining operations are outside your premises. This means a quiet, cool home.

- No additional energy costs.

- You will not be stuck with costly equipment should miner stop being profitable.

- You will not experience any ventilation problem.

- There is very little chance of being let down by equipment suppliers.

The Cons of Cloud Mining

Cloud mining can sometimes be a risky option. Some of these risks are described below;

- Mining operations are opaque in nature and lack transparency.

- There is a risk of fraud.

- Reduced earnings as profits are split and costs have to be paid.

- There is a general lack of control and flexibility.

Avoiding Cloud Mining Scams

Investments in cryptocurrencies have grown immensely in the last one year. Plenty of small term investors earn a recurring income through cloud mining. Here are a couple of things to watch out for.

1. Must have ASIC Miner vendor support: Ideally, any legit miner will voluntarily and willingly let you know about their provider and IT support firm they are dealing with. If a company does not have such support, then it probably is suspicious.

2. Data Center and mining equipment photos: A genuine cloud mining operation should have photos of its data center and mining equipment on its website. Any firm that cannot show you photos of its operations is honestly not worth investing in. Some companies even show proof of electricity bills, so you should not take any excuses from companies that do not provide photos.

3. Check for presence of mining address: Any legitimate cloud mining company is likely to display its public mining address. Many of the legitimate ones actually do, like Genesis Mining. If the firm is unable to provide one, then it most likely is not genuine.

4. Take a look at the company's registration: Genuine cloud mining companies often have every clear registration with proper domains and are open. They should never be anonymous as they are supposed to be very open with members or investors. Full contact details, for instance, are absolutely essential. When these are missing, such as an official address, phone number, and so on, then it is probably a scam so avoid such a firm.

5. Watch out for referrals: Cloud mining sector makes thin profits because there are many members who have to be paid as well as certain costs such as electricity, rentals and so on. As such, they cannot afford to have referral programs that pay 5% or 10%. Any cloud mining firm offering to pay such high fees to affiliates is probably not genuine so take your money and run.

6. Be cautious when they offer guaranteed profits: In cloud mining operations, profits or income are never guaranteed. However, a scammer will try all ways and means to lure you into their scam. Also, some companies provide no option to withdraw your earnings. This is actually absurd. You should be allowed to withdraw your earnings whenever you want. Firms with opaque payment systems and those with unclear withdrawal processes should be avoided like the plaque. Please keep off such websites to avoid losing your money.

Basically, there are plenty of red lights to watch out for. You need to be comfortable with a company's profile and image. If you have any doubts or feel like something just does not add up, then your instincts are probably right. Make sure you find only genuine companies, check the reputation and reviews online and if you feel confident enough, you are probably right.

Guaranteed Returns in Cloud Mining Operations

If you join a cloud mining firm, you will enjoy certain benefits. While you are likely to get a return on investment in a couple of months, it is not possible to give a certain guarantee of return on investment. The reason is that cryptocurrency mining relies on a couple of factors, one of these being luck with regards to market prices for your chosen coin.

Since luck is a factor in mining, getting a return on investment is not always guaranteed. It is possible to earn a good return every day over a long period of time. It is also possible to finally recover your initial investment. However, no cloud company should give you a guaranteed return as it is not in control of the entire process. If you join a reputable crypto mining company, then you are likely to make your money back and keep earning a residual income for some time. Not all companies are able to provide you with the kind of return you would want.

List of Noted   Mining Scams to Avoid

There are a number of cloud mining programs that are Ponzi schemes masquerading as legitimate mining operations, or have already been proven to be Ponzi schemes. Many of since shut down, but unfortunately, some are still running to this day. Below is a list of some of the schemes you can avoid.

1hashmining.com - Ponzi scheme pretending to be a mining operation. Update: The website has now been shut down by authorities

50BTC.com - A mining pool that stopped paying out. The host's whereabouts are currently unknown.

7cly.com - A mining scam that promises returns of 2% per day. You should know by now that this just isn't realistic in any market.

Minerjet.com - Another one with guaranteed returns promised. Stay well away.

Mininghub.io - Another cloud mining operation. This one has a made up UK limited company behind it. Avoid like the plague.

Store4mining.com - A website claiming to sell mining hardware. They don't, only use trusted sources to purchase mining equipment.

Bc-prime.com - This one was actually running Google Ads for a while so even the world's biggest search engine thought they were legit. Fake mining platform which will steal your cryptocurrency.

Bitcoin-mining.group - This and all subdomains (which are focused on other coins like XRP) are fraudulent.

Bitminer.world - This one makes you send in more Bitcoin if you want to withdraw your earnings. Absolute sham high yield Ponzi scheme, and an utter disgrace to the mining world.

An Introduction to Mobile Mining

It is possible to mine cryptocurrencies using your mobile phone. There are apps in the market available for android smartphones that can mine cryptocurrencies. However, it is a challenging prospect as mining operations require a lot of power and consume huge quantities of energy.

Bitcoin and Ethereum mining operations require mining rigs. They consume huge quantities of energy, so such operations can hardly be performed on your smartphone. The only possibility of mining these major coins is to get one of the latest and most powerful smartphones in the industry then connect it to a mining pool. Therefore, mining the way we know it using a mining rig is not possible via smartphones.

Mobile Mining Apps

There are certain apps that you can download that will mine cryptos for you. These are mostly android apps so if you have a powerful smartphone, think about downloading one of these apps and begin mining immediately.

1. DroidMiner BTC/LTC Miner: This is a bitcoin mining app that lets you mine cryptocurrencies if you connect to a pool. It connects to the Get-Work pool. It is only through the pooling of resources that smartphones can actually mine altcoins such as Ethereum. Droid Miner is an Android based tool that was developed by ThatGuy. The architecture of the DroidMiner is based on Pooler's CPuminer and AndLTC Miner software.

Apart from Bitcoin, you can also mine Litecoin and Dodger Coin. In fact, it can mine all coins that use SHA-256 or scrypt. There are currently just under 500 users mining with this app and they give it an average rating of 3.5 out of 5.

2. Easy Miner: The Easy Miner is yet another pool mining application program. This app is easy to use, comes with an improved user interface, and displays crypto charts showing the latest prices. It also displays the network's hashing rates, so you are always aware of the mining situation.

3. LTC Miner: This is yet another android app that can be used to mine cryptocurrencies. It is specifically designed to mine within the Litecoin pool. You can easily join the pool and earn Litecoins on a regular basis.

While these apps are great for pool mining, they are still not suitable for actual mining using your phone's hardware mining just yet. Not until android develops much faster hardware will you be able to profitably mine on your phone.

MinerGate Mobile Miner

MinerGate is a mobile mining app for android phones. With this app, you can turn your smartphone into a portable mining rig. This was developed by an ordinary crypto miner who submitted it for a contest. It was such an impressive app that it was immediately adapted for use.

You first need to download the app onto your smartphone and then set it up. Once it is set up and ready to use, simply open an account with your details then log in. Now all you need to next is choose your preferred cryptocurrency. Simply find the coin you want to start mining and click on it.

Once you identify your preferred currency, simply start mining and earning. Ensure that you have a mobile wallet attached so that your earnings are storied in there. You can always check the balance any time you want. You can also see which currencies you are currently mining because, apparently, you can mine more than just one crypto.

Even as you mine, you are given plenty of options. For instance, you can choose to mine only when your smartphone is charging, or request mining to stop when the battery is low. You can choose to mine on the go so that you connect to the pool and mine coins as you go about your day.

Top Crypto-Mining Apps for Android

People all over the world are mining cryptos on their phones. They are mining Dogecoin, Bitcoin, Litecoin, and Ethereum among many others. If you want to start mining coins on your smartphone, then you can consider one of these apps. They are considered among the top android apps for coin mining.

1. BTC Safari

2. Bitcoin Farm

3. Easy Miner

However, before choosing an app to use, it is advisable to do your due diligence, learn more about the app before investing in one. Like previously stated, Bitcoin mining is not as profitable on your cellphone, so I'd recommend against any Bitcoin mining apps. You are better off mining smaller altcoins on your smartphone rather than Bitcoin.

How to Make Money Staking Coins

You can earn cryptocurrencies through a process known as staking. Many cryptocurrency investors are now looking at alternative investment streams and staking is certainly one of them.

What is staking? Staking is also referred to as Proof of Stake.

Proof of Stake is a concept where you buy coins and store them in your wallet for a given period of time, say, three months. It compares well with putting money in a fixed deposit account. You can save money in a fixed deposit account for a couple of months or weeks and then earn a decent return at the expiry of the said period.

Basically, Proof of Stake has so many technical benefits to any network. However, apart from these, investors also enjoy some economic benefits. They get to earn dividends by staking their coins in a particular wallet. Essentially you can make money by simply holding many POS (Proof of Stake) coins in the right wallet. This wallet is referred to as the staking wallet.

The system appreciates PoS because it helps secure the network and keep it stable. It also creates additional opportunities for network users to earn dividends based on their coins.

Understanding Basic Staking Terms

Distributed consensus: The term distributed consensus refers to a large group of investors who live in vastly different regions of the world but have a unifying agreement. In the world of cryptocurrencies, the agreement is mostly on the blocks or transactions that are valid and should be added to the network.

Proof of Stake: This is a specific algorithm that is used by some cryptocurrencies to manage their distributed consensus. It compares to Proof of Work and is considered a better alternative for achieving the same consensus.

Most Profitable Proof of Stake Cryptocurrencies

1. DASH: This cryptocurrency is also known as digital cash and is a very popular coin. It is among the first to introduce Proof of Stake and is built on Bitcoin's core but with better security and added privacy features.

Dash does have a higher barrier to entry at 300 DASH to run a masternode, which gives 7.5% annual interest.

2. OKCash: This is yet another cryptocurrency that makes use of Proof of Stake. All you need to do is buy some of this currency and store in a stake-able wallet. OKCash currently has a 10% annual return for staking, with no minimum amount required, which makes it advantageous when compared to Dash for example.

3. NAV Coin: NAV Coin is among the first cryptocurrencies to operate on a dual blockchain. It's been in operation since 2014 and uses Proof of Stake for block verification and stability. You can use POS stake rewarding on this coin to earn extra cash regularly. This also enables you to earn even as you sleep, with an annual return rate of around 5%.

4. ReddCoin: ReddCoin is very popular on social media networks. You can use this POS based cryptocurrency to leverage content on social media to get handsome returns.

5. Stratis: This is another POS coin that you can use to stake and earn rewards. STRAT is the token that operates on the Stratis platform. You will, therefore, need a Stratis wallet to stake your tokens. While profits are not quite as high as with other coins, with time, this is expected to get better.

6. Neo: My personal favourite staking opportunity. Neo is similar to Ethereum in that it uses what is known as Gas (similar to Ether) to keep the network running. Unlike other Proof of Stake currencies, Neo doesn't require you to keep your wallet open at all times for staking.

Currently you require around 20 Neo to return 1 Gas, which represents an annual dividend of just less than 6%. The bonus with Neo is that as more applications run on the Neo network, the more Gas is needed, and thus your Gas is worth more. So you actually get a 1-2 punch of higher Neo values plus higher Gas values. This is what makes Neo my personal favourite of the staking coins.

Examples of Initial Investment vs. Expected Return on Investment

Remember that Proof of Stake operates in an almost similar manner to fixed deposit accounts. For fixed deposit accounts, you are paid an interest after maturity of the deposit. However, for Proof of Stake, the rewards you receive are crypto tokens.

1. The longer your coins are held in the staking wallet, the higher the rate of return. For instance, you receive 20% return after 3 months, 50% after 6 months, and 100% after a year. Thus the rate of return will depend on the maturity period.

2. The rate of return is sometimes calculated as simple or compounded interest.

Let us say you invest 100 ETH in a staking wallet for 3 months. At the end of 3 months, you will expect to earn 20% more ETH. This means you will own 120 ETH in that period of time.

(100 * 20/100) + 100 = 120 ETH

Please note that you can only stake with altcoins and not Bitcoin. Bitcoin rewards miners through the algorithm known as Proof of Work.

Advantages of Staking Crypto

The benefit of staking crypto is that you will not need to invest in expensive mining equipment. All you need to do is buy the coins you need then save them in a staking wallet. Then just sit back and watch your investment grow. It is a pretty decent, safe, and lucrative way to make money.

Another advantage of staking is that you get to have a predictable, secure, and guaranteed income. This is because the value of the coin increases predictably and its value at maturity can easily be determined. Staking does guarantee you will get your investment back.

Mining based stocks - An often overlooked opportunity

What if you could profit from cryptocurrency mining, without having to mine yourself? It's true, it's completely possible.

Two of the biggest cryptocurrency winners in the past few years, haven't been cryptocurrencies themselves, but ones that are affected by the boom in cryptocurrency mining.

You see, mining cryptocurrency requires a huge amount of computing power, in the form of Central Processing Units (CPUs) and Graphics Processing Units (GPUs). Manufacturers of these parts have seen their stock prices skyrocket since the beginning of 2016 when cryptocurrency mining really took off.

AMD ($AMD) and NVIDIA ($NVDA) are the two biggest winners thus far, in fact, in Q3 2017, NVIDIA's revenue from mining soared to $220 million for the quarter. Now, nearly 5% of the company's bottom line is attributable to cryptocurrency mining. AMD, on the other hand, sees roughly 10% of its overall revenue being from cryptocurrency mining sources.

The companies themselves have different approaches to how cryptocurrencies will affect their profits going forward. AMD CEO Lisa Su stated that they were expecting a "cryptocurrency cooling off period" in 2018, and the company doesn't consider demand for GPUs as a part of its long term gameplan.

NVIDIA, on the other hand, is more bullish and has openly admitted that it considers cryptocurrency mining a big part of future business plans.

So if you're into traditional investing as well as cryptocurrencies, it may be well worth checking out both of these stocks and seeing if they have a place in your portfolio.

Another Cryptocurrency Lending Scheme to Be Wary Of

In my previous books I have warned readers about BitConnect and DavorCoin, both of which are lending platforms that promised users guaranteed returns on investment. Like the regular financial world, you should be extremely skeptical of any platform that promises guaranteed returns. Since those books were published, both of these platforms have performed exit scams and taken thousands of dollars (millions in the case of BitConnect) from users. BitConnect and those who promoted it is currently in the process of a lawsuit for fraudulently acquiring assets. The same fate may well happen to DavorCoin.

In the meantime, however, there is a third lending platform that has been making waves recently in the shape of FalconCoin. According to their website, users will receive daily interest on coins with the monthly interest rate being 46%. That figure alone should have your alarm bells ringing because 46% interest in a month is a frankly absurd figure. The other big red flag is that investments must be locked up within the platform for a minimum of 180 days before users can withdraw them. They also claim you'll be able to "earn 180% by staking Falcon Coins".

Like these other lending platforms, FalconCoin, of course, has a referral program and is aiming to use social media to spread the word. This is what caused BitConnect to get extremely popular as larger YouTube channels (such as CryptoNick and Craig Grant who are both named in the BitConnect lawsuit) were advertising the project to their followers, who would sign up under their referral links. Referral programs don't necessarily mean a project is bad, however, if that ends up being the main source of income, as we see with many MLM/pyramid schemes, then we indeed have a problem. Through a few minutes of research, I already found multiple YouTube channels that were promoting FalconCoin and encouraging their viewers to sign up under their particular referral code.

Overall, FalconCoin displays the exact same red flags as BitConnect and DavorCoin before. Guaranteed returns and promises of ridiculously high interest rates are just too big to ignore, and as such, I would advise anyone to stay well away from the project.

Conclusion

Thank you for reading, and I hope what you read was informative and able to provide you with all of the tools you need to achieve your cryptocurrency mining goals, whatever they may be.

I encourage you to do additional research on top of what you've read here. Especially with regards to mining specific cryptocurrencies, as the procedure will be different for each one.

The next step is to find the best website where you can apply all the wonderful knowledge obtained through this book. Mining cryptocurrencies is a lucrative way of earning an extra stream of income, and many people just like you are making a decent secondary income from doing so. While this might not be your golden ticket to early retirement, who can say no to an extra few thousand dollars a year?

Remember, stay away from mining and lending platform scams. And with any investment you do make, only invest what you can afford to lose.

Thanks,

Stephen

P.S. If you want to buy cryptocurrency, and haven't done so yet. I recommend Coinbase as the easiest way to do so.

If you sign up for Coinbase using this link, you will receive $10 worth of free Bitcoin after your first purchase of more than $100 worth of cryptocurrency.

http://bit.ly/10dollarbtc

Cryptocurrency: What you need to know about your taxes to save money and avoid a nasty surprise from the IRS

By Stephen Satoshi

Introduction

OK, so you've been buying or trading cryptocurrencies for the past few months or years and now you want to know exactly how this affects your tax situation.

To be frank, a year ago I had no clue either, so I did a research deep dive, contacted various institutions and people of note and found something fascinating...no one had any idea how it all worked! In fact, in 2015, the IRS discovered that only 802 people in the entire United States had declared any cryptocurrency related gains or losses on their tax returns. This has led to the IRS demanding Coinbase hand over customer records, which we will expand on later on in this book.

Fortunately, in the past 12 months, we have had some concrete developments in cryptocurrency tax laws. Now we have the ability to at least construct an outline as to how this all works, and what exactly you are liable for when buying and trading cryptocurrencies.

I should note this is **not** tax advice. Everything expressed in this book is my own personal opinion and nothing more. Please contact a tax professional before you submit your tax returns.

One more thing, the content here is focused on the US market, your local tax laws may well differ.

Anyway, let's get cracking shall we?

Stephen

Some important things to know at the outset.

Early data from credit monitoring firm Credit Karma shows that less than 100 people out of a sample of 250,000 filings, actually reported cryptocurrency gains or losses on their tax return last year. This amounts to just 0.04% of the sample size paying their cryptocurrency taxes to the IRS. While obviously not all of those doing the filing would have held cryptocurrency, it's safe to say the actual number is a little higher than 0.04% of all American citizens. The latest estimates have around 7% of US citizens owning cryptocurrency in one form or another.

In another survey of 2,000 cryptocurrency owners, 57% said that they realized gains on their coins, but an even higher number (59%) stated that they had not reported any gains or losses to the IRS.

This combined with other factors like online tax providers (such as TurboTax) not integrating cryptocurrency taxation shows up that it's not just the citizens who are behind on crypto taxes, it's the authorities and tax based businesses as well.

What this tells us is that people, in general, are confused about how exactly they should file their taxes for cryptocurrency and therefore, more education in this area is needed, and that's what I hope to be able to provide in this book.

Let's start off with the basics, shall we? What class of asset does the IRS consider cryptocurrencies to be exactly? Well, you may be surprised to learn that cryptocurrencies are not considered securities or stocks. Therefore there are a large number of tax laws that do not apply to cryptocurrencies. But there are an equal number of laws that *do* apply and make this is a rather complex issue. So if you're getting excited and thinking that crypto is "tax-free" then think again.

So what are cryptocurrencies considered? Well according to IRS note 2014-21, any digital currency, or in their own words "virtual currency" is considered "property" for tax purposes. It should be noted that at the time of writing, this is the only official statement the IRS has made about cryptocurrency. Oddly enough, the Securities and Exchange Commission (SEC) made a contrary ruling in 2017 when they decided that cryptocurrencies *were* indeed a currency.

The IRS ruling means your cryptos can be considered business property, investment property or personal property. In practical terms, and the big thing to note here is that any gain or loss is recognized every single your exchange your property, in this case, cryptos, to purchase goods or services.

Therefore if you're somehow who pays with cryptocurrency frequently, then you may well have more tax preparation to do than someone who merely buys and holds, or exchanges their cryptocurrency for fiat. This can make for an accounting nightmare if you haven't kept track of your cryptocurrency purchases. So I would advise you to do that as a bare minimum going forward.

The reason for this is that the IRS considers this two separate transactions. The first of which is the sale of your coins, and the second of which is using the proceeds of that sale to make a further purchase. Therefore, if you've bought Bitcoin at any time before January 2018, then it has most likely increased in value, and thus you will have to pay capital gains tax on it.

Let's use an example. You spend $4,000 on furniture at Overstock.com and you pay using Bitcoin (Overstock was actually the first major retailer in the US to accept Bitcoin as a method of payment). Using November 2017 figures, we'll say that Bitcoin was worth $8,000 at the time of the transaction, so you spent 0.5BTC on the furniture.

Now here's where it gets confusing, if you bought your Bitcoin back in early 2016 when BTC was trading for just $200 a coin, then you have a capital gain of $3,800 ($4,000-$200). Using the standard capital gains tax rate of 15% you have a $570 tax bill on your hand.

However here's where it gets even dicier. Even you spend your Bitcoin or any other cryptocurrency within a year, then you may be subject to the short term capital gains rate of 39.5% (this rate is scheduled to fall to 37% in 2018). This is on the top of the sales tax you have already paid for the goods themselves, so you're essentially undergoing a double tax hit.

This has huge ramifications not only on a personal level (no one wants to be taxed twice) but also on a widespread cryptocurrency adoption level. And we haven't even begun to discuss how this affects day traders, how can make multiple cryptocurrency transactions per day. We'll expand on this point later on in this book.

We have to remember as well that this is the IRS we are talking about. One of the most powerful institutions not only in America but in the entire world. The fact of the matter is this - if they want to find you, they will.

However, there are moves to make things easier for those who like to pay with cryptocurrency. A bi-partisan bill has been introduced by representatives that would only require you to report cryptocurrency purchases with a value of greater than $600. This makes more sense going forward, but it remains to be seen just how quickly this becomes written into the tax law.

How does my tax bracket relate to capital gains?

The formula for this simple for long term capital gains. So if you held your coins for a period greater than 12 months. It should be noted that these tax brackets are federal tax brackets, you state income tax level does not affect your capital gains.

People in the 10% and 15% tax brackets pay 0%.

People in the 25%, 28%, 33%, and 35% tax brackets pay 15%.

People in the 39.6% tax bracket pay 20%.

Hypothetical Scenarios:

Julie bought 1 Bitcoin on March 4th, 2017 for $1000. She then sold her 1 Bitcoin for $3000 3 months later on June 4th. Therefore her taxable gain is now $2,000.

If she was in the 15% tax bracket she would pay $300 ($2000*15%).

If she was in the 25% tax bracket she would pay $500 ($2000*25%)

If she was in the 39.6% tax bracket she would pay a whopping $792 ($2000*39.6%)

But say Julie keeps her Bitcoin for 1 year and sells on March 4th, 2018 for the same amount of $2,000. Her capital gains now look like this.

If she is in the 10 and 15% tax she bracket pays $0

If she is in the 25%, 28%, 33%, and 35% tax brackets she pays $300 ($2000*15%).

If she is in the 39.6% tax bracket she pays $400 ($2000*20%)

So by keeping her Bitcoin for a year, she saves almost $400 in taxes for the exact same transaction. So if you have no reason to sell (and remember, cryptocurrency is a long term investment so unless you literally need the money to eat you have no reason to sell), then you are better off keeping your coins for over 1 year to trigger the tax savings.

Now there is no way of telling if the price of cryptocurrency will be greater or less in one year than it is today. But if you have long term belief in the technology behind cryptocurrency, and thus its long-term viability as an asset as opposed to a short-term speculative vehicle, then it is well worth holding onto your coins.

What about if I sell for a loss?

If you have sold cryptocurrency for a loss at any time, this is, of course, deductible on your tax return. This is known as an "above the line" deduction, in the same way that interest of your student loan is deductible.

It should be noted that the maximal in capital gains losses you can deduct each year is $3,000. This is proportional to your income in the same way capital gains is. If you have more than this then you can roll it over to the next year until the remainder is cleared.

So for example, if you buy Bitcoin at $10,000 and it crashes to $5,000, at which point you sell, then you have a loss of $5,000. You would be able to deduct $3,000 in this tax year and then $2,000 in the next tax year, provided that these are your only losses.

What if cryptocurrency is re-classified as a foreign currency?

This is a perfectly plausible scenario. If this were to happen then any gains would be exempt from the capital gains tax, and more important there would be no more short term capital gains penalties. You would simply be taxed at your regular tax rate. This has a particular benefit to day traders who are currently at the mercy of short term capital gains rules.

However, there are additional advantages in the case of transactions for goods and services. Under the foreign currency exemption for personal transactions (so not business or investment ones), gains under $200 are tax free. If cryptocurrencies continue to be adopted on a consumer level, where the vast majority of the day to day purchases will be under $200, then this will be a big win for those who like to spend their coins.

The biggest issue we have in cryptocurrencies gaining foreign currency status is that because they are not minted or produced by a foreign bank - are they technically foreign at all? I would err on the side of caution for now, and go by the rules that the IRS has in place.

What if my job pays me in cryptocurrency?

This will only apply to a small percentage of readers, however, that percentage is increasing at a rapid rate. Year by year there are more and more people working in exchange for crypto. This especially applies to those working on ICO projects who are paid in tokens by the founders in lieu of fiat currency.

Luckily, the way you calculate taxes for services rendered is pretty simple. If you sell goods or services (such as your own skills) for cryptocurrency, your tax basis is their fair market value at the time your cryptocurrency was received.

So if you received 10ETH for a project when ETH was $500=1ETH then your tax burden would be the equivalent of $5000. Obviously, you should always keep track of the date you received your coins. You should also be consistent with which exchange you use because choosing multiple exchanges for the benefits of better rates is unfortunately going to run foul of IRS regulations.

What if I haven't sold my coins yet?

OK, so assuming you haven't sold any coins or traded them for any other coins. You have simply bought them for fiat and held. Then you would have zero tax events and you do not have to report anything to the IRS. Once you do sell or trade those coins, then it becomes a tax event and you would have to report any gains or losses made. So if you're a pure HODL'er, then don't worry about anything just yet, the IRS will only want to know when you sell your coins.

Let me make one thing clear at this point. **This is the only way to avoid realizing gains.** Any other suggestions are just patently false.

It should be noted that once you do sell them, it doesn't matter if you keep the money on an exchange or if you cash it out to your bank account. It still counts as sold at the time of sale. So you can't get around the IRS by keeping your money in Coinbase for example.

What if my friend/family member/dog gave me cryptocurrency as a gift?

I would be willing to bet that cryptocurrency gifts were at an all time high last year and that more people received Bitcoin, Ethereum or Litecoin in 2017 than in all other years before them combined.

What you need to be concerned with is the basis of these coins when they were purchased. Hopefully, there has been a capital gain in the time when the gifter purchased them for you and when you received them.

The confusing part of this is if they were purchased for a higher price than their value when you received them. So in other words, if you have inherited a loss from the gifter. In this case, you can use the value at the time you received them, not at the time of purchase. This particular regulation leads you to have the best possible tax situation with gifting.

If you haven't sold yet then you don't need to worry, but this does affect you when to do decide to sell. So as unflattering and impolite as this may be, it's worth asking your friend their purchase date and the purchase price of the coins that have gifted you. This will ensure any future filings are indeed correct.

Let's do a few examples to clarify this.

Steve buys 1 Bitcoin for his friend Mary at $1,000. By the time Mary receives them, they are only worth $800. So to begin with, Steve's basis is $1,000 in this situation.

Scenario 1 - Mary sells for at $1,200. As she has profited, she inherits Steve's basis of $1,000 and she has a capital gain of $200.

Scenario 2 - Mary sells at a loss for $600. She cannot inherit Steve's basis so uses her own of $800 so her capital loss is $200.

Scenario 3 - Mary sells for $900. She still cannot inherit Steve's basis and a loss, so she uses her own for $800. Therefore her capital gain is $100, however as it is less than Steve's basis, it does not have to be reported as a gain or a loss.

The sale can be disregarded in this case, because there is no gain from the initial basis. This is all very confusing, which is why it is vital that you get the purchase price and purchase date from whoever gifted you the coins.

What if you are the gifter?

Like other gifts, giving cryptocurrency as a gift is not a taxable event because the recipient inherits the tax basis. So don't worry if you bought Bitcoin or Ethereum for your family and friends this holiday season, you're in the clear. Of course, if you exceed the gifting limit ($14,000 for 2017 tax year) then obviously you will have to file. Note that if you are married and you and your spouse file together, you can give up to $28,000 or $14,000 per person.

There is also the lifetime gift exemption of $5.4 million but obviously, that doesn't apply to the vast majority of readers.

How does the IRS know about my cryptocurrency?

Well, this question isn't easy to answer, the short answer is that someone told them. Don't worry, there are no crypto snitches out there reporting you without your knowledge. There are a number of ways this can occur.

The most common is that the IRS requests the data from an exchange. They can do this with exchanges based in the US, and also exchanges based in countries which share tax treaties with the US. The biggest one of these is obviously Coinbase, and its sister site GDax, which is based in the US and is therefore subject to the demands of IRS.

They would report you gains in the form of form 1099-K. We discuss under what circumstances a 1099-K would be filed by Coinbase later on in this book.

The second way, and probably the most common way for the regular investor would be if your bank account was flagged for one reason or another. This is known as a Suspicious Activity Report (SAR) and many banks will file one of these because of cryptocurrency transactions. Banks tend to be cautious types so many times they will file a SAR based on frequent cryptocurrency transactions or transactions for large amounts. There is no hard number for the filing to be enacted but you can safely assume that any single transaction over $5,000 has triggered this. Obviously, the larger and more frequent your transactions, the more likely you are to be flagged. It should be noted that SAR filings are often done to avoid money laundering investigations so you shouldn't be worried if one is filed against you. Just pay the amount you owe and you can go on your way.

The third way is that you volunteer the information to the IRS yourself. Now there are significant penalties for failing to report income, so I recommend you report your gains within the appropriate reporting period. Now if you're behind, don't worry too much because the confusing nature of cryptocurrencies may well lead the IRS to be more lenient in this particular domain, but it goes without saying that you should file any back taxes as soon as possible.

The fourth and final way is indeed if someone reports you. If you're the kind of person who has a lot of enemies this is somewhat plausible. But for many it won't apply. One lesson you should learn is to not brag or discuss large cryptocurrency holdings you may have, because people can and do get jealous, and as such, one may report you. This applies even more so on public internet forums where the information can potentially be seen by thousands of people.

How to invest in cryptocurrencies tax-free

This is a big one that many investors overlook because it's not very well published, and your regular accountant probably isn't even aware of it. But the good news is it's pretty simple and easy to execute even for a technophobe.

It is completely possible to add Bitcoin, Ethereum and other cryptocurrencies to your retirement portfolio such as your IRA. It goes back to the IRS ruling we discussed previously where cryptocurrencies are ruled as personal property. Therefore the IRS doesn't consider it to be "collectible" and as such, there is no limitation in adding it to your retirement account.

There are two ways to invest in crypto using an IRA

The first of which is to use what is known as a "captive" IRA, so basically your provider will buy the cryptocurrency on your behalf and then you can store and access it as you wish. This is similar to how most IRAs work and if you use a financial advisor to handle your retirement affairs you will likely be familiar with the process. The drawback of this is that your account handler may not directly buy cryptocurrency and may instead buy an alternative form that is executed in cash, such as purchasing shares of the Bitcoin Investment Trust which actually trades Bitcoin at anywhere between a 20 and 50% premium in relation to its actual market price.

The second way of doing this is a self-directed IRA. If you already have an IRA dedicated to holding real estate or other alternative asset classes, you may be familiar with this one. The advantage here is that you will directly own your cryptocurrencies yourself. However these types of accounts are trickier to set up and therefore you must ensure you get everything right the first time round, or otherwise, you may get into hot water with the IRS down the line if everything is not in order.

To set up a self directed cryptocurrency IRA you must have your cryptocurrency stored in a wallet, in other words, not on a cryptocurrency exchange. However, this cannot be a personal wallet so you cannot use a hardware wallet like your Ledger Nano S for example. Thus you must work with your provider to set up a separate wallet which is purely for your retirement funds. I would seek advice from your provider to ensure everything is set up correctly.

The other option is that you can create a separate LLC for the sole purpose of holding the wallet and then be responsible on the balance sheet for all transactions in and out of the wallet. If you haven't done this before I wouldn't recommend it for a first timer, because the added complication of a cryptocurrency wallet can make it confusing to those without experience in the area.

FBAR Requirements

Now the FBAR applies to income stored outside of the United States. If you ever held more than $10,000 outside of the USA on a single day you are required to file your FBAR online. How this affects cryptocurrency is if you have ever had more than $10,000 worth of coins or cash on an overseas exchange, then you must file. This particularly affects those who trade regularly on Binance or other non-US based cryptocurrency exchanges, and have held a significant amount of money on there.

OVDP & Streamlined Domestic Offshore Disclosure

Note if you suspect you are not compliant with these regulations for the previous year,s you can file an IRS voluntary offshore disclosure and get back into the IRS' good books. The best way to do this is with the Offshore Disclosure Volunteer Program (OVDP), this program is designed to facilitate compliance with the IRS and the DOJ. The program is open to any US taxpayer with offshore holdings or financial accounts. The main requirement for this program is that you are not currently under IRS investigation. The reason for the previous necessity is that by being a voluntary program, you must not be "forced" to enter it and if you are already investigation than that would constitute force. The standard OVDP application includes 8 years of tax return filings and 8 years of FBAR statements as well as other supporting documents.

The second one of these programs is most applicable to most people who this ruling affects. It's known as the Streamlined Domestic Offshore Disclosure. Despite it's strangely contradictory name, it deals with foreign accounts and foreign held money. Once again, contact an offshore disclosure attorney if you do wish to file.

If you have a significant amount and are behind on declarations, I would recommend investing some of that money and hiring a well experienced offshore disclosure attorney.

What about coins that were airdropped or I received as part of a hard fork?

Like most other cryptocurrency related tax issues, hard forks are a confusing one. According to Robert Crea from law firm K&L Gates "It's something new—it doesn't fit neatly into a dividend or stock split or even mining."

Crea's colleague Elizabeth Crouse then explained what this could mean for your tax liabilities.

"From the IRS's perspective, whenever you get something new you didn't pay for, it's accretive—it's income," she says. "When the Bitcoin Cash shows up in someone's account, that's probably a taxable event. The question is what's it worth."

As seen above, the main coin in question that we have to look for here is Bitcoin Cash (BCH). As a result of a hard fork, anyone holding Bitcoin on August 1st received an equivalent amount of Bitcoin Cash.

The question now is whether you would have to report this to the IRS and pay it as a capital gain, based on the price at the time of distribution (roughly $277 per BCH). Or the other scenario where you would only pay based on when you sold BCH.

The IRS is yet to make an official judgement on how exactly airdrops work though, and when contacted by various news agencies, simply referred back to their initial statements that conclude that cryptocurrency is considered property.

In this case, you would have to report your income based on the price of the coin at the time. In other words, just because you got your BCH for free, doesn't mean the IRS considers it to have zero value. In other words, it's a taxable event.

Now this gets dicey for those of your holding your Bitcoin in a Coinbase or GDax wallet because you would have received your Bitcoin Cash on January 1st, 2018, when the value of Bitcoin was much higher.

The other big hard fork event, that will affect those of you who have been in the market for longer, is the July 2016 Ethereum hard fork when Ethereum holders received Ethereum Classic (ETC) as a result of the hard fork after the notorious DAO hack.

Then there is the case of air drops. Many coins over the past few years have airdropped into wallets on certain exchanges. Tron, for example, airdropped 500 TRX into Liqui wallets in September 2017. With this example, you inherit the cost basis of the "gift" at the time you received it. As many of these air drops had little value at the time you received them, it won't be an issue for the IRS. This is unlike BCH which did have significant value at the time it was distributed (approximately $277 per BCH), which is more likely to trigger a tax liability.

Of course, once again this only applies when you sell your coins. Simply holding them is not a taxable event.

Can I actually pay my taxes *in* cryptocurrency?

Is it possible to minimize your tax burden by paying in Bitcoin or Ethereum? Does the IRS accept crypto as a form of payment? Unfortunately, the answer to both of these questions is a resounding no. The IRS does not currently accept tax payments in anything other than US dollars.

However, at a state level, there may be some changes to this. For example, Arizona is the first state looking to pass a law that allows its citizens to pay state income taxes in Bitcoin as well as other sanctioned cryptocurrencies. This follows the lead of a number of municipalities in Switzerland which passes laws allowing their citizens to pay taxes in cryptocurrency.

If the bill passes it will be introduced by 2020 at the earliest so we're still a little ways off. Interestingly enough, the legislature states that Arizona would not hold the payments in cryptocurrency after they are made and would convert them back to fiat for their own use.

It is an encouraging sign though and we may well see other states follow suit in this respect. I would hesitate to think that federal allowance of tax payments in cryptocurrency is any way close though due to the increasingly complicated nature of passing federal laws versus state laws.

What do I do if I haven't reported anything thus far?

OK so first things first, relax. Unless you have holdings ranging into 6 figures, it's unlikely the IRS or any other government agency is going to come kicking your door down.

Your best option depending on your holdings would be to contact a good tax attorney and accountant. If you do have significant holdings (6 figures plus), and you haven't been compliant for multiple years, I would urge you to spend more money and hire the best you can afford, because it will make the process a lot smoother going forward. The IRS is not an organization you want to mess around with and therefore you should absolutely do your utmost to be compliant.

Also, be wary of any company that promises cheap and quick offshore incorporation as a means of hiding assets or lowering your tax burden. Many of these companies can and will set up foreign bank accounts for you, but just because your money is going into a foreign account, does not mean you do not have to pay tax on it, as is the often misquoted information online.

Thirdly, everyone's situation is different, there is absolutely no one size fits all solution for this and thus do not believe everything you read on internet forums or social media. A good tax attorney and accountant is the only way you will truly get accurate information for *your* situation.

If you have low level holdings of only a few thousand dollars then you can still self report. Remember to keep track of all your crypto transactions, and if you haven't done so already, start doing this going forward.

Does taxation affect the price of cryptocurrencies?

This issue came to the forefront around December 2017, when a lot of first time crypto investors and traders realized that tax season was coming.

Therefore, there was a lot of speculation that tax season was actually affecting the day to day price of crypto. While some believed that many investors were pulling their money out of the market after December 31 but before January 31st to in order to pay their taxes, and spread their burden across multiple years. Others simply speculated that it was a coincidence and that the US market isn't the biggest player in the crypto world. However, a similar pattern has emerged for the past 3 years so the theory may well have some merit.

What is interesting is that this is actually a different pattern to the stock market which tends to do well in January as institutional investors reestablish their positioning as they move into the new year. Either way, it's an intriguing pattern to monitor going forward.

Needless to say, you can't let short term price fluctuations like this affect your long term investing strategy, so unless you are a day trader then it's best not to worry about minutia such as this.

What about ICOs - are they tax-free because they are used to raise capital?

While this would make sense and would be in line with the 2017 SEC ruling that cryptocurrencies are a currency, the answer is actually no.

While conventional capital raising methods are considered tax exempt by the IRS. ICOs don't work in the same way. Therefore the proceeds of an ICO will be considered taxable income. The amount would be determined by the value of cryptocurrency received (in other words, the donation cryptocurrency rather than the new token) on the date the ICO ended. So if your ICO received 1000BTC and it ended when 1 BTC was worth $1000. You would have $1,000,000 of taxable gains.

The other thing to note is that unless you formed a corporation before you begin the ICO, you will be personally liable for the gains received. Obviously, if there are co-founders like most ICOs then you are considered a partnership for tax purposes and you will be responsible for an equal share of the net income made from the ICO.

Therefore if you are a developer and are planning to conduct an ICO then you should definitely consider forming a corporation beforehand. Income will then be taxed at a corporate rate rather than a person rate which has far reaching benefits for the people involved.

One interesting thing to note is that by conducting your ICO earlier on in the tax year, you may be able to acquire some extra benefits such as being able to spend the proceeds on deductible expenses. This includes operating costs, salaries and other items like office rent.

There is a lot of speculation that forming an offshore company can have a number of tax benefits, especially when it comes to legally avoiding US taxes. Needless to say, offshore tax laws are extremely complex, depending on various factors such as the jurisdiction where your incorporated the company, your tax residency and a myriad of other factors. They are difficult for even a seasoned tax accountant to navigate, so ensure that you have everything straightened out before you decide to go this route.

Beware of companies offering quick fix solutions like incorporation and bank account set up offshore, many of these companies will tell you that you will be completely compliant with US tax, but then you can find yourself in hot water down the line when it turns out there were certain things they *didn't* tell you in regards to your personal tax status. Often their advertising will use easy selling points like "0% tax rate", but it would be wise to investigate this fully before you do pull the trigger on any arrangement.

This is especially true if you reside in the US, then your income from an offshore company will still be subject to US taxation. Foreign owned companies will also have to deal with FBAR requirements that we previously discussed in an earlier chapter. You also have state taxes to be concerned with as your state will probably want some of your gains as well.

What if I make capital gains one year but lose the money the next year?

Here is a tricky situation, but certainly something we should all be aware of in the case of a market crash. If you make gains in one tax year, you will be required to pay them even if you make large losses the following year.

This can be troublesome in the case of a large year-long correction or bear market like we saw in 2015. There were a notable number of investors who made large gains in the prior year but as they expected this to continue, didn't take profits and kept much of their holdings in cryptocurrency. They went on to make some serious losses the following year and by the time their tax bill was due, they found they didn't have the money to pay it.

Obviously, we can't predict the way the market is going to go, but we can take some steps to ensure that we aren't left out of pocket. The biggest lesson from all this is that you should take intermittent profits for yourself no matter how good the market is doing because trust me, you'll thank yourself the next year if the market does take a turn for the worse. Make sure you can cover any tax burdens, and don't leave it to the last minute to withdraw your money because chances are a lot of people are doing the same thing, and thus it could cause a short term dip.

There are some exceptions to the rule but these will be made on an individual basis by the IRS themselves. So if this does apply to you, and you believe you could qualify for one, I recommend speaking with an accountant and seeing what can be done about your situation.

How are my cryptocurrencies taxed if I mined them?

Yet another area in which there is no real hard legislature right now is in the field of cryptocurrency mining. The IRS has made one ruling on this in Notice 2014-21 Q9 which states that anyone who mines cryptocurrency is "subject to self-employment tax on income derived from those activities."

In terms of how much your mined cryptocurrency is actually worth, the official IRS ruling right now is that each coin mined is given the value that it had when it was awarded on the blockchain itself. In other words, the value on the day it is mined, is the basis for that coin going forward.

For example, if you mine 1 Bitcoin when the value of BTC is $500, then its basis going forward is $500. So if you then sell it for $700 a year later, then your capital gains is $200.

When it comes to the subject of expenses and electricity, mining expenses are deductible if you have incorporated yourself into a mining business. Obviously, if you are a mining business, electricity would be a significant proportion of your monthly expenses and therefore there is no reason at all why they would not be a legitimate deductible. It should be noted that you will also have to make note of the square footage of the room your mining rig is housed in, as this is often how electricity expenses are factored when there is a multi-use situation. It should also be noted that you cannot write off electricity for an entire room (like your living room) just because there is a mining rig housed there. Trying to do this is an easy way to get the IRS on your case. Other mining expenses such as depreciation of your mining rig and its parts would also be deductible.

If mining is just a hobby for you, you must still pay additional self employment tax on any amount earned which is greater than $400 in a single year.

Gains made from mining pools or cloud mining would be subject to the value of your payouts as well as money initially invested. Once again, consult a tax professional to get a better handle of the situation.

However, on a strict consumer level, this is probably not a deductible. This is quite a gray area and I would recommend speaking to a professional for greater clarification on this subject.

Are crypto-to-crypto transactions considered "like kind" exchanges?

This is where it gets murky, although the logic would dictate that these kinds of transactions are indeed "like kind" exchanges and thus would not be a taxable event, this officially is not the case for the time being.

Unfortunately, the guidance from the IRS regarding this is over 3 years old now, when cryptocurrency and high volume cryptocurrency trading was far less common. So at the moment, we will have to treat crypto-to-crypto exchanges as not being like kind and therefore every single trade will be a taxable event.

So what does this mean for your returns? It means that any gains or losses can be written off against each other for that particular year, but cannot be moved over to another year. So for example, if you make $20,000 in capital gains one year, you cannot use these to offset a $10,000 loss the following year.

The other important thing to note is wash-sale rules. Designed so that traders do not fraudulently claim losses, this applies more to cryptocurrency than you might think. Wash-sale applies if you sell an investment at a loss, then re-invest in that same asset, in this case, the same coin, within 30 days of investing.

Let's do an example.

Say you buy 1 bitcoin at $20,000, it dips to $10,000, then eventually surges to $25,000. You sell 0.2 BTC at $5,000, which is a capital gain of $1,000 which you'd be responsible for short term capital gains tax.

However, if instead, you sold your bitcoin when it hit $10,000 and repurchased it, you'd reset your cost basis to $10,000 and claim a $10,000 loss on taxes.

When the price increases to $25,000 and you sell your 0.2 BTC, it would be a $3,000 capital gain, but combined with your paper loss of $10,000, you'd still be looking at a $7,000 capital loss. For wash-sale rules to apply, all these trades must have occurred within a 30 day period of the initial purchase of Bitcoin.

Wash-sale rules currently only apply to stocks and securities, which cryptocurrencies are not considered as the IRS labels them as property. So in theory you could apply these to your tax return and benefit.

However, under regular tax law, you would have to prove these trades were done for some other purposes other than just to benefit on your taxes. This is known as the Economic Substance Doctrine, so it is completely plausible that the IRS would not allow you to use these as a tax write off. The IRS uses this to fight against illegal tax shelters that long use this trick to provide additional tax benefits for their owners.

You can use the idea of market risk to argue to the IRS that these losses were sustained as a result of market volatility and nothing else. This is because the IRS considers you personal economic benefits at risk rather than just the potential tax benefits. Of course, any transactions over the 30 day period would not run afoul of any of these rulings and thus you don't need to be concerned with them if that is the case.

The Coinbase Form 1099-K

We discussed this earlier in the book and now we'll cover it in grater depth. You may have received a form from the IRS in the mail within the past 3 months, this was likely Form 1099-K which relates to your cryptocurrency holdings which you **sold** in exchange for fiat value within the past tax year.

If you have received this it is likely that you have had a Coinbase account for a period longer than 12 months, and your sales of cryptocurrencies exceeded $20,000. The $20,000 number is based on federal law that third parties must report sales over this number to the IRS. Therefore, this is a form that Coinbase has to send to the IRS, as it strictly relates to transactions on third party networks. So in this case, it will only include transactions on Coinbase and its sister website GDax.

This form does not give the IRS an indication of your total cryptocurrency holdings, or those on other sites outside of Coinbase or GDax. Nor does it give the IRS access to your wallet address on those two websites.

The one thing to note is that the form relates to your gross payment amount. This particularly relates to traders, especially day traders making many transactions. Therefore every single transaction is recorded and totaled up. In the case of Bitcoin, if you sold BTC at $10,000 twice - this would trigger the $20,000 threshold, and thus you may well have received the form, even if your net gains were well below this amount. This will also *not* take any transactions fees into account.

So if you sold your cryptocurrency for a loss, it would not take this into account. Therefore don't be surprised if the payment amount on the form is higher than your actual trading gains.

Let's do an example:

January   - you buy BTC at $8,000 and sell for $7,000 (a $1,000 loss)

February - you buy ETH at $500 and sell for $1,500 (a $1,000 gain)

March - you buy LTC for $1,000

The number on the form would be $8,500 ($7,000+$1,500), which is higher than your actual gains. This form only relates to the sale amount, so your purchase amounts won't even be displayed and thus the IRS does not have data into your actual trading profits.

It should be noted that if you have not received one of these forms but have been trading significant amounts, then it is your responsibility to file a 1099 form to the IRS. You won't be able to use the excuse of "I thought Coinbase would do it for me" either, it's very much up to you to take the initiative in these kinds of dealing with federal tax authorities.

How to generate transaction reports on Coinbase & GDax

If you're a frequent trader and you do make a lot of transactions, when you have to file your taxes, you'll need to make sure you note down every single one of these transactions. It will make it a lot easier to you square things away with the IRS.

Below is a step by step guide on how to find an accurate number of all your cryptocurrency transactions in the past year using Coinbase & GDax.

Instructions for Coinbase:

1. Click "Tools"

2. Click "Reports" in the sub menu

3. Click "+ New Report" button

4. Set Account to "USD Wallet…" and Time Range to "Last Year"

Instructions for GDax:

1. Navigate to the menu in the top right

2. Click "Accounts" in the sub menu

3. Click "USD Account" in the menu on the left

4. Click "Download Receipt / Statement"

5. Set Time Range to "Custom" from 01/01/2017 to 12/31/2017

How can you minimize your cryptocurrency tax burden?

So first things first, this applies to regular investors rather than frequent traders, who obviously will not be able to take advantage of many of the tax laws here. I should also note I am talking about legal ways to lower your overall tax bill. Not illegal ways to avoid paying tax.

The big one is to hold on to your coins for at least 12 months after you buy them. This will allow you to be in the long term capital gains bracket which will always be below 20%, whereas the short term capital gains will be taxed at the same rate as your regular tax bracket.

The second one is mainly for peace of mind purposes, but try to use as few exchanges as possible so it's easy for you to track all your trades. Being able to download your entire trade history from Coinbase or GDax is very simple, but other exchanges, such as EtherDelta, do not have any trade records at the time of writing. It's unlikely that the IRS will accept "well the website doesn't record trades" as an excuse, so try to use exchanges where you can have a record of all your trades where possible.

As previously mentioned as well, if you received coins as a gift that are now worth less than their value when you received them, you will be able to write some of these off as a capital loss. So ensure when you receive them you discuss with the gifter the date they were purchased and the value of the coins at that date.

Depending on your income bracket you may also be liable for an additional 3.8% Net Investment Income Tax. Consult the IRS website for further details.

Can you register yourself as a self-employed trader to get a better tax deal?

There are a number of advantages to being a self-employed trader in the eyes of the IRS. The main one being, if the IRS considers your trading a "business" then your gains and losses become ordinary.

Registering a trader is extremely difficult though and your registration must be renewed twice a year to qualify for the benefits. There are a number of advantages and disadvantages to doing this. The may disadvantage being that your losses are no longer deductible because this is considered part of your day to day business and thus regular capital gain rules no longer apply.

However, just being on Binance a lot is not going to cut it come tax season. So if you do want to register yourself I would recommend consulting a tax professional if you want to go this route.

What about altcoins with no official conversion to fiat

In the case of many altcoins that don't have direct fiat trading pairs, you would use the USD value of the fiat equivalent that you traded them for. For example, if you bought 50XMR for 20 BTC and that 20BTC was worth $10,000 at the time, then officially you bought $10,000 worth of currency during that transaction.

This applies when you go to sell as well. It doesn't matter if the final sale was against another altcoin or not, the transaction will be recorded in US dollars. Obviously, this represents a great difficulty for a lot of people, so if you have been trading frequently I would seek out professional help from a tax firm.

Were there any changes in the crypto tax laws between 2017 and 2018?

So as we previously stated, there has only been 1 official ruling on cryptocurrency by the IRS. This was back in 2014, and nothing much has changed since then.

So like-kind exchanges still apply, you will pay taxes on crypto-to-crypto exchanges when you eventually convert these to fiat. Obviously this implication will have more effect on frequent traders and day traders then your regular buy and hold investor.

There are new federal tax brackets, which will affect your capital gains and these are listed below.

Rates for Individuals in 2018.

10% - Up to $9,525

12% - $9,526 to $38,700

22% - 38,701 to $82,500

24% - $82,501 to $157,500

32% - $157,501 to $200,000

35% - $200,001 to $500,000

37% - over $500,000

Rates for married couples filing jointly

10% - Up to $19,050

12%- $19,051 to $77,400

22% - $77,401 to $165,000

24%- $165,001 to $315,000

32%- $315,001 to $400,000

35%- $400,001 to $600,000

37%- over $600,000

How are other countries dealing with cryptocurrency taxes?

While we wait for US tax law to evolve to be at a happy medium with cryptocurrency gains, it is interesting to see just how other countries are handling the problem.

Germany, for example, considers cryptocurrency to be foreign currency and trading in cryptocurrencies is considered a private sale. They also do not have any long term capital gains tax on cryptocurrency, so if you buy 1 ETH on June 1st 2016 and sell it for a profit on June 1st 2017, then you would not have to pay any tax on your gain.

Denmark is another progressive crypto country. In its goal of making the Nordic nation the world's first cashless state, cryptocurrency trades are not taxed and there is no capital gains on Bitcoin either.

In January 2018, the Portuguese tax authorities announced they would not be levying any taxes on profits made by trading cryptocurrency. The government of Belarus also announced that as of March 2018 there would be no taxes on cryptocurrency for its citizens for the next 5 years. This is to encourage the adoption crypto as well as to promote blockchain and smart contract technology. Serbia is another nation that is completely tax free for cryptocurrency profits, including profits made from crypto mining.

However, other countries are less friendly towards their citizens' bank accounts when it comes to cryptocurrency, for example, in Germany the short-term (less than 1 year) capital gains tax can be as high as 46%. In France, the situation is even worse and this number can top 60% in some cases.

Then there's the rather bizarre case of the few select crypto millionaires who are trying to construct their own "cryptocurrency utopia" in Puerto Rico. By establishing residency on the Caribbean island, which is a U.S. territory, they are aiming to avoid state and federal taxes. Puerto Rico has become somewhat is a tax haven in the past decade due to no federal personal income taxes, no capital gains tax and favorable business taxes — all without having to renounce your American citizenship. Which makes it an ideal tax haven for any US citizen.

There are talks of many of these men building lavish mansions with their own docks and airstrip for private planes. These men include Bryan Larkin, a crypto billionaire who was one of the early adopters of Bitcoin mining with an estimated personal fortune of around $2 billion. Another notable figure is Reeve Collins, one of the co-founders of the controversial US Dollar tether, which is a cryptocurrency pegged to the value of the US dollar, used for exchanges between altcoins. Needless to say, the project is in the early stages still and many of the group spend the majority of their time drinking at hotel bars rather than building mega mansions. It will definitely be interesting to see if it ends up as a cryptocurrency utopia or if the opposite happens and it turns into a Lord of The Flies situation.

Conclusion

Well there we have it, I hope I've cleared up some questions and that you've come out of this book with more knowledge about the general cryptocurrency tax situation than before.

We've covered everything from capital gains and losses, to how mined cryptocurrencies are taxed as well as gifting. We've also gone over the different forms that are filed and the various ways the IRS will be aware of your cryptocurrency tax situation, so I hope I've been able to address the vast majority of concerns you had before buying.

Remember, everyone's personal tax situation is different, and there is no one size fits all solution, no matter what anyone tries to tell you. It should be noted that anyone trying to tell you that their one size fits all solution works for you, is probably just trying to get your money.

If you have a single take away from this book, let it be this. The only person who will be able to help with your own situation is a qualified accountant or tax attorney. This is one area I would recommend paying more money and hiring the best you can afford, especially if you have made a lot of more with crypto.

I wish you the best of luck in your ongoing cryptocurrency journey. We all hope the IRS can get a better grip on the crypto tax situations as we go forward, but it may well be a few years before we get some better guidelines and more streamlined processes. In the meantime, just make sure you keep up with tax compliances and file on time every year.

And as always, I hope you make a lot of money with cryptocurrency and that it affects your life in a positive way.

Thanks,

Stephen